THE WEIGHT OF FEAR

ONE WOMAN'S JOURNEY FROM FEAR,

TO FREEDOM, TO FORGIVENESS

A MEMOIR BY

TAMMY HIGDON STEBBINS

Dedication

I dedicate this book first and foremost to my honey, my husband, Jeff.

To my children, Adam and Crystal—my greatest gifts of all

To my grandchildren—Layla, Molli, Alex, Ava, Lexi, Alizabeth, Connor, and Graham—my heart

To my sisters—Ann, Janie, Vickie, Mary—my truest friend and editor,

June —my Heavenly partner in crime,

Linda (a.k.a. "the baby")

To Jim Hisle —who never gave up on me.

To Jim Parks and Bart —each the very definition of a friend.

To Robbie and Austin—my forever angels.

And to my brother, Jerry—may he finally be at peace

AUTHOR'S NOTE

Writing this memoir has been a journey through a difficult past, that was encased in poverty, fear, mental torment, and violence. Each step of the journey has increased my awareness of how the events of my past have shaped the person I am today.

I do not claim to capture every detail exactly as it occurred but acknowledge that the memory of my life experiences has been distorted by the passage of time and the influence of layers of trauma. It is an honest recollection detailed to the best of my ability. Names have been changed to protect the privacy of some individuals.

My hope is that within these pages you will find the inspiration to embrace the person you've become, confront your past with strength and courage, and find peace and ultimately freedom, through forgiveness.

Tammy Higdon Stebbins

TABLE OF CONTENTS

Introduction

In 2014, my sister, Mary, was sponsored by a friend to take part in a spiritual retreat. She spoke about the experience a few times, never going into detail, simply saying that it had changed her life. I never pressed her for specifics, believing she would share more if she felt the need. I had all but forgotten about the event when Mary asked if I'd be interested in attending the retreat—mentioning that she needed an answer soon, as the paperwork deadline was quickly approaching.

At first, I was unsure. This wasn't the kind of thing I would typically say yes to. But after some soul searching, I decided it might be time to wander outside my comfort zone. I cleared my schedule and told her I would love to go. Mary not only sponsored my retreat but also took care of my transportation to and from the retreat. I spent the weekend with about fifty women, growing closer to Christ and experiencing a kind of love I hadn't felt before—genuine, honest, and free of expectations. It was simple and real, and it stayed with me.

When the retreat was wrapped up, Mary returned to drive me home. She asked me if I had gotten anything from the retreat. As we secured my bags and I settled into my seat, I turned to her and said, "I did get something out of this weekend, I have decided I'm going to write a book." Her response was simple but firm; "I think you should." I needed to consult some people about the idea, as I recognized the potential to reopen old wounds and even create new ones. My intention was not to harm, but to create a path for healing. It was after much thought that I decided that before I could begin this journey. Quite frankly, some people had to die

My parents carried the shame and guilt of our past for over forty years, and I would not have added to that suffering. To bring the harsh truth of our family secrets into the light would have been unbearable for them. They had passed on years earlier and no longer carried this heavy burden. But they weren't the only ones I felt the need to protect. There was also my abuser, the person I resented more than anyone else in the world, my brother Jerry. Despite the pain he inflicted, the damage he caused, and the trauma that continued to weave its way through my family, I could not bring myself to cause him further suffering. He had suffered enough.

Jerry moved to Florida after our mother's death in 1992 and remained there until 2024. At the time I made the decision to write this book, he was very ill. His health had declined due to years of alcohol abuse and the stress of his mental illness. His children feared it was only a matter of time before his body gave out. They were right. He passed away in March 2024. Once he was resting peacefully in a place where the retelling of these events could no longer harm him, it was time to tell the story, his story and mine. One cannot be told without the other, as they are intricately interwoven. In January 2025, I finally put pen to paper.

This book is not about religion. I am not a religious person. I am simply a child of God. My faith does not come from communion with others, nor has it been strengthened by the Word delivered from a man behind a pulpit. I enjoy and see tremendous value in both. But my faith has proven unshakable because of the undeniable evidence I have witnessed ~~throughout my life~~. This book is not about survival. I am not a survivor; I am merely surviving. This book is not about revenge. That is not my battle to fight. But if anything defines me, it is this: I am a fighter. And a fierce one. A wise man, one who is dear to my heart, once told me, "Tammy, don't win the battle just to lose the war." That hard-won piece of wisdom became a compass for me through countless moments where pride begged for a fight. It has spared me more times than I can count.

I was born into a world that did not want me, a world where struggle was a given and violence was a way of life. Another little girl was another mouth to feed, taking up space, adding to the chaos. Hunger was a looming threat, and children were not spared its cruelty. I was one of eleven children living in a house too small for the thirteen bodies crammed inside it, and with walls too thin to keep out the cold. But those walls were able to contain years of secrets.

Survival was a lesson learned before speaking in sentences. Survival meant speaking only in a whisper, keeping your distance, never making eye contact, never attracting attention, never sitting in the wrong chair, never walking in front of the TV, never slamming a door. And always knowing where to hide. Survival meant never showing emotion and never revealing your pain.

LINDA AND ME

Little girls, three, four, and five years old, knew these rules and followed them. Little girls, barely walking, learned that walking on eggshells is painful to little feet and can leave permanent scars. The scars were not exclusive to the little ones. The older brothers and sisters experienced their shares of physical and emotional wounds. Even Mama and Daddy suffered unimaginable treatment that made their children yearn to protect them.

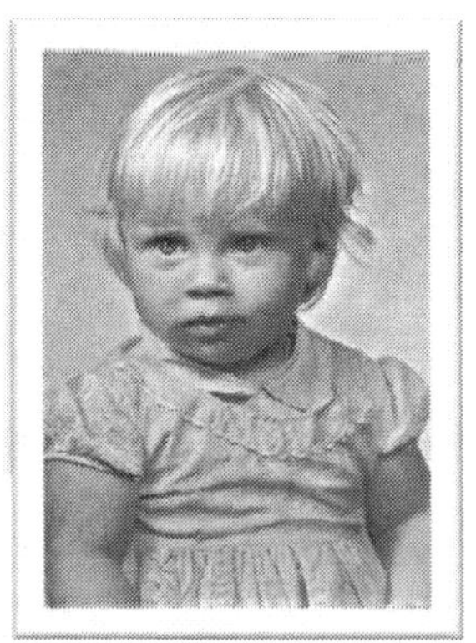

LINDA AT AGE 2

Golden curls tangled from days of play without combing, tiny feet blackened from going barefoot as much by choice as by necessity, and handmade dresses bearing the stains of long wear. Night after night, small bodies climbed into bed, sliding between sheets stained from bedwetting and streaked with grime from our bare feet. The fabric, worn thin by years of use, held quiet evidence of childhood and poverty. The scent of sweat and sleep and urine hung in the air. Who could steal the innocence of little girls burrowing beneath their covers, squeezing their eyes shut, holding their breath, and pressing close to one another for comfort. Who could do such a thing?

SISTER WEEKEND- SUMMER 2018

I learned early that love was a thing between sisters and fear could fill the stomach when food did not. The weight of fear settled deep inside me, shaping the way I moved through the world. Even after its source was no longer a threat, the years of damage remained. Trauma had carved itself into my memory, leaving me struggling to break free from a prison that I had already escaped. Fear was my constant companion throughout childhood and remained so, long into my adult years weaving itself into every part of me. It defined the way I interacted with people, and despite my relentless fight to protect those I loved, its reach extended across generations to the people I cherished most, the ones I had a duty to protect. My children and grandchildren were not spared its grasp, and this only added to my guilt.

SISTER WEEKEND- WINTER 2014

The Family

MAMA AND DADDY ON THEIR

WEDDING DAY-APRIL17, 1944

I was born Tammy Crystal Denise Higdon in the small town of Wax Kentucky to John Robert Higdon and Mary Jessie Idean (Deanie) Alvey Higdon. Mama and Daddy were married on April 17, 1944, and remained married for forty-eight years before mama died in1992. Their marriage would produce twelve children.

LARRY'S CLOTHING AND GRAVESTONE

Larry Robert Higdon was born March 4,1946, and died on July 27, 1946. Mama never spoke of her first born. We learned from Mama's sisters that Larry was born blind and never cried. Larry died in the middle of the night and Mama woke up in the morning finding her baby beside her, obviously deceased. She sadly believed that she had killed him by rolling over onto him in the night. No one could convince her of anything different. Daddy once told us that Larry slept in a pulled-out dresser drawer, but that night Mama went to sleep feeding him.

Mama kept a small box that held two dresses that she hand-stitched for Larry and a tiny hat daddy made for him from one of his old hats. They are precious, delicate reminders of a short, silent life. That box and a small tombstone in the cemetery of our childhood church, a quiet reminder of his brief existence, is all we have ever known of our first brother. The weight of grief must have been heavy on my Mama's frail shoulders. She took that weight to her grave.

JERRY IN 1959 AT THE AGE OF 12

Jerry Denis Higdon was born in 1947. There is little known of his early years. A few photographs remain that show a smiling Jerry riding a bike or pleasantly posing for a school picture. In 1966 he was drafted into the army and was sent to Vietnam. He was nineteen at the time. While he was away, Mama knelt by a chair in her bedroom every night, fingers moving steadily over the worn beads of her rosary, whispering prayers for his protection and safe return home. She was often found alone in her quiet room softly crying, her tears falling unnoticed in the silence. When Jerry returned from Vietnam, he was not the young man who went away two years earlier. He carried home with him a shadow; something unseen but deeply felt; a presence that embedded itself into the walls and lay thick in the air of our house, lurking in the dark corners, waiting.

At first my older brothers and sisters believed Jerry's transformation stemmed from the weight of his memories from the war. The things he had seen and done resulted in a disturbing change in him. But as the years passed, the darkness did not subside. It grew stronger, more intentional, more diabolical. While in our home the laughter of children grew quiet and a stillness fell over our lives like a heavy blanket, holding us captive with its weight and promising to slowly leave us all sharing the last breath of air. For forty years this presence remained. It was undeniable, unnatural, unholy. We tried to escape it, to bury it away in the back of our minds. But some wounds do not heal with time, and some ghosts refuse to be laid to rest.

Christopher Edward Higdon (Chris) was born December 15, 1949. He was named after our maternal grandfather. Chris was reserved, pleasant, and humble. He married in 1971 at the age of twenty-two to Connie who was fifteen at the time. They had two children. Chris was a bricklayer by trade and took great pride in his work. He was constantly making improvements to his own home, mostly to benefit an animal or to make room for someone in need of a place to sleep. He loved animals like they were people. He built birdhouses all over his property. He kept chickens, rabbits, cats, and dogs and a goose that I know he ordered straight from hell. That damned goose would chase a person all over the yard and Chris would just stand there and smile. He rescued a dog that had one leg missing. His young daughter, when speaking of the dog, would say that he only had four legs.

Chris and Connie took in any stray that came along. That included human ones. They adopted a young lady, Connie's niece, who quickly became part of our family. She died of cancer at a young age, leaving behind a husband and a small child. They also adopted a great nephew, Jerry's grandson. Chris and Connie were married for forty-four years when they separated. Their differences regarding the raising of their adopted son proved to be more than their marriage could survive.

Mauritia Ann Higdon McClure (Ann) was my caregiver for most of my preschool years. She babied me and took care of me like I was her own. One night mama and daddy were away from home, probably having a baby. The only reason they ever left the house for any length of time. Ann suddenly stood up from the table not knowing that I was right behind her and scooted her chair right into my chest forcing me into the wall. Protruding from that wall was a finishing nail. The back of my head slammed into the nail sending blood running down my scalp and onto the floor. Ann was terrified, thinking my injury was much worse than it was. She cried and pleaded with me to forgive her, but I milked it for all it was worth. I still use it against her when the opportunity presents itself and Ann, being the kind hearted person she is, the opportunity presents itself often.

Another memory of Ann that is carved into my mind was being awakened in the middle of the night by several screaming voices. I can still see Ann standing at the edge of the yard in her nightgown holding onto the clotheslines and then buckling to her knees and sobbing. Mama let out an animal like wail and ran toward her. One of my sisters sheltered me from the scene by guiding me back to bed, telling me that Ann had taken too many pills, but she promised, "She is going to be okay." Soon after, an unmarried Ann gave birth to a son. He was a welcome light to our perpetually dark home.

Magnora Elaine Higdon Childress (Janie) married young. She left home still bearing the scar the size of a silver dollar where Jerry violently slammed a door on her kneecap. Janie was a tough one. It was rare for Jerry to cross the line with her because she had a mean right hook and zero tolerance for his crap. This time, he caught her with her back turned leaving the scene of the argument. She left home, like most us girls, for a safe place where she didn't have to fear going to sleep at night. She soon learned that life with her husband would be no reprieve from the constant fighting at home when she became the outlet for his rage.

Despite living only a few miles from her family she was forbidden to have any contact with us. That isolation began after a violent showdown between Daddy and Janie's husband—one fueled by Daddy's fierce disapproval of the way his daughter was being treated. Words flew first, then fists. Though she lived close to us, it was as if she'd vanished. Her husband didn't just isolate her. He cut her off completely. We weren't allowed to see her, speak to her, or even know how she was doing. I remember the headlights beaming across our front porch. I remember the sound of the engine starting. I remember the terror of seeing my daddy being struck in the face. And I remember the moment Janie was dragged by her hair, screaming, to the car, while we stood frozen. One minute she was home. The next she was gone. And she did not leave, she was taken.

Bell Vickie Marie Higdon (Vickie) was always Mama's favorite. Vickie married young but continued to spend most of her time with Mama. She had a little boy while living at home which was nothing less than her heart's desire. She married a few years later and soon gave birth to her second son. She and her new husband moved a good distance from us, forcing her to spend more time in her new home and less with Mama. She remained Mama's favorite and had no problem telling us that. Vickie dedicated her life to her children. She was completely selfless when it came to their needs. Whatever the situation, her children always came first.

Charles Freelon Higdon (Freelon) was always different from the rest of his family. He aspired to do more than what was expected of the Higdon children. Freelon began to take karate in his early twenties and had a third-degree black belt in record time. He could take a running start and run up the side of a tree, turn a flip and land on his feet. He could hold a tree or post with both hands and extend his body and hold himself in a complete horizontal position. He became involved in a Protestant church and departed from the Catholic way before any other member of the family even dared to think about it. This was like a slap in the face to Mama and she had no qualms about showing it.

Freelon had a refreshing sense of humor and loved to outsmart his siblings at every opportunity. He was also a no-nonsense person. He suffered the wrath of Jerry like the rest of us, but he became less of a target as he got older and turned out to be more of a threat to Jerry. Freelon tried to teach me some karate which was like trying to teach a cat to talk. Freelon was a loner. He did his own thing. He stayed to himself. I always looked up to him for this reason. I liked being around him just soaking up his energy. He could be dismissive at times but occasionally he would indulge me with a game we just came up with one day when he allowed me into his room. I thought I was the most important person on the planet when he agreed to play the 'cassette game'. He had an impressive collection of cassette tapes. The game would begin with him playing a song off one of the cassettes, then letting me try to guess which cassette the song came from. I was wrong most of the time but one time I was right. I still remember the time I guessed correctly. It was the song, "In Through the Outdoor," by Led Zeppelin. It was one of the proudest moments of my young life.

Mary Jean Higdon Embry (Mary) was born on November 28, 1958. Mary was my idol. I watched her and tried to emulate her kindness, her independence, and her strong will. Like Freelon, she reached for higher stars than most of our family. Just after high school she got a job and bought herself a car. That was a huge deal in my family. She made her own clothes and did her best to keep the house presentable. She married at nineteen to a local dairy farmer who pursued her until she caved. They lived on a large farm that we all loved to visit and did so often. Their home was an Oasis, a safe place for us younger children and Mary and Wayne always welcomed us and provided the comfort and protection we so badly needed. They were married for forty-two years and had three children before he died of cancer in 2020.

Mary always had an awareness of the needs of others. Linda recalled one night at dinnertime when Mary demonstrated her compassion for her sister."It was a time when food had been scarce for a period and Mama was really struggling to put dinner on the table.

Someone had given us some ground beef and Mama stretched it out enough to make one burger for each of us. I ate mine very quickly, and before I had even swallowed my last bite, I looked at Mary and asked if she was going to eat the rest of hers. She was holding it, ready to take a bite when I asked. She handed it to me and said, “No. I'm full. You can have the rest.” For years I carried tremendous guilt over that day knowing that I took food that Mary needed just as much as I did. I have learned to let go of the guilt as I was just a child. But hunger is a potent force, and the memory of that hunger is still vivid, the pain still sharp. I believe that will haunt me for the rest of my life.

June Marie Higdon Pierce (June) was born October 9,1962. June and I were quite different as young girls. She was adventurous and fearless. She had a shock of red curly hair that would give a tumbleweed a run for its money against a comb. Mama would not even touch June’s hair. That deed was left for daddy who showed a surprising amount of patience for the task. Children quit school before the legal age of sixteen frequently in those days and for any number of reasons. June was probably in a league of her own, quitting to avoid the daily torture of daddy’s comb.

One day Ann and her husband, Bobby, were visiting with us. Bobby asked for a cup of coffee and June, and I were both determined to be the one to give it to him. We grabbed the last clean coffee cup together. We poured the coffee together, and we both carried it into the living room together. When we handed it to Bobby, the tugging back and forth caused us to spill a bit on his leg. Daddy responded swiftly by landing a slap on June's cheek. She just happened to be the one closest to him. I let go of the cup so she could do the honors of handing it to Bobby. Daddy's slapping her did not sit well with me. I may have wanted June to disappear off the face of the Earth, but I was not going to stand for someone else mistreating her. I took her hand and whispered in her ear. "We are running away".

We grabbed one of mama's quilts, a quart jar of water, and leftover biscuits from a plate on the stove, and traveled the twenty yards to the barbed wire fence. We threw the quilt over and spread it out in preparation for an extended stay, leaving mama and daddy searching the neighborhood for their lost little girls. An hour later, we were hightailing it back over the fence to the home we once knew, sadly admitting that we hadn't even been missed and continued hating each other once more.

ME, AGE 3 AFTER MY CLOSET HAIRCUT

When I was around three. June took me into the closet and proceeded to cut my hair with Mama's sewing scissors. Mama recalled hearing giggling coming out of the closet. She opened the door to find the closet floor covered in blond hair. Guess who's. June had cut my hair to the scalp in some places. A four-year-old in a dark closet trying to finish a job before Mama caught her. I am lucky my hair is all I lost. According to Mama, she grabbed me out of the closet and took me to Daddy and asked him to buzz my hair so that it could grow back even. I know my Mama and I know if she opened a closet and found June, and me, and her sewing scissors there, she was going to grab her scissors and shut the door. She had one pair of scissors and eleven kids. For years. When June wanted to scare me, she would look around to make sure no one was listening and she would quickly whisper, "Want another haircut?"

June worked as a server for way too many years and retired at fifty-five simply because her body was giving out on her. Within a few years, she was diagnosed with brain cancer. Thanks to the wonders of modern medicine, we were given another two years with our beautiful June, and she died with all her sisters surrounding her and singing her favorite song, "Sylvia's Mother", by Dr. Hook and the Medicine Show.

I stood at June's left side, my hand resting under her head. I felt the weight shift and I knew she was gone. One of her last wishes was to be bathed and dressed in fresh clothing when she left her house for the last time. As my sisters prepared her body for the ride, my mind wandered to January 2008. June, Freelon, Vickie, and I had tickets to see Dr. Hook in Owensboro. We were beyond thrilled at the chance to see these guys in person. We wore out our Sloppy Seconds CDs and waited with eager anticipation for the night to arrive.

I was living in Breckinridge County and the three of them lived in Clarkson. I planned to meet them in Owensboro, see the concert and then spend the night at the Executive Inn. My car was packed and ready when I woke up the morning of the big day. As I headed to the kitchen for a cup of coffee, I was quietly singing the words to "Freaking at The Freaker's Ball". I poured my coffee and sat in my favorite chair by the window. I pulled back the curtain and nearly dropped my coffee when I jumped to my feet screaming. "Nooooooo". A thick blanket of snow covered the ground, the driveway, and the roads. Jason came into the room to see what the commotion was about. When I informed him of my plans for the evening, he stated that the roads were impassable, even for his four-wheel-drive truck. I was forced to call June and tell her I was not going to make it to Owensboro. She was as disappointed as I was but assured me that she, Freelon, and Vickie were sticking with the plan.

The next morning, I spoke with June on the phone. Still buzzing with excitement, she recalled the events of the night before. The crowd at the concert was minimal due to the weather. This allowed her to move to a table directly in front of the stage. Ray Sawyer, the lead vocalist, spoke directly to individuals in the audience. When he learned that my family drove more than an hour in the snow to attend, he asked June to come up on stage during one of their songs where she danced with the band leader and even got a kiss on the cheek from him. She had photos to back it up. I was sick thinking about what I had missed and knowing my chances of catching Dr. Hook in concert again were slim to none.

Linda Rose Higdon—the baby, my little sister, my greatest ally, and sometimes my fiercest rival was born on August 1, 1965. Being so close in age, we shared everything: clothing, shoes, makeup, and much to my annoyance, we even shared identities in the eyes of others. We looked so much alike that people constantly confused us, calling me Linda and her Tammy. Every gift we received was labeled, "To Tammy and Linda," as if we were a single entity rather than two separate people. I remember growing increasingly frustrated by that, yearning for something that was just mine.

Sibling rivalry ran deep between us, especially as we entered our teenage years and began sharing a room in our new home. We argued over clothes, space, privacy, who got to use the mirror first in the morning, and, of course, boys. Even when we got along, there was always this underlying tension, a silent competition simmering beneath the surface. But despite all of that, Linda was my best friend.

It became a running joke in our family that I couldn't even go to the bathroom without yelling for her to come with me. We bickered constantly, yet no one else was allowed to mess with her. I could tease her, fight with her, and call her names, but if anyone else so much as looked at her the wrong way, they had to answer to me. She was my partner in crime, my constant companion, and the one person I could always count on. No matter how much we clashed, Linda had my back, and I had hers.

JEFF AND ME, AGES 5 AND 9

Jeffery Dean Higdon (Jeff) was born August 1st, 1967. He was, of course, Mama's baby in every way. He spent most of his time sitting in her lap. He was probably the first baby that mama was able to really spend time with. By the time he was born all the older sisters were taking care of the younger ones and Mama had some time to breathe. The chaos and violence in our house took a toll on Jeff.

By the time he was four or five, he was already showing signs of anxiety, constantly wringing his hands and biting his lip. The cards were stacked against him from the beginning. Despite all of this, Jeff was a good-natured, well-behaved little boy. He never got into any trouble except for things like putting a frog in one of our drinks or saying the occasional curse word. He asked Mama, after one of his slips, if he could have just one bad word to say when he got mad. Mama thought about this and leaned over and whispered something in his ear. She had allowed him to say "shit" when he was really mad. He started to get mad a lot and Mama took his bad word away. He was not Daddy's favorite. All the attention Mama gave him did not set well with Daddy. He thought she spoiled him, and she did, thank Heaven.

Jeff started smoking marijuana in his early teens. In his late teens he pretty much moved in with a friend to escape the turmoil at home. He married young and had a son. He was in no condition to raise this child, and our sister took him in and raised him as her own. Jeff moved away, remarried, and now has a daughter that is the light of his life. His drug use escalated to the point that he was homeless. Austin Wooden, our Chief of Police, found him out in the middle of a field one day in an old, abandoned car. There are things about that situation that I don't think about or talk about. It is too painful so it will have to remain a mystery. Jeff is drug free today and has been for many years, but the physical and emotional stress left him a walking ghost physically. Mentally, he tries to stay on the sunny side.

ME AT AGE 3 IN FRONT OUR HOME IN WAX, KY

Our little house in Wax, Kentucky was the first on a dirt road called Prancy Ridge. Our's was a small, cracker-box house with a living room, kitchen, and three small bedrooms. The house was basically just a shelter. The walls had half-inch gaps, letting snow drift in in the winter and the rain in the spring and summer. The house was always in ill repair. When it rained, we placed buckets and kettles throughout the house to catch water leaking from the ceiling. We even had buckets in the middle of some of our beds. I remember miserably pacing the floor at night waiting for the rain to stop so that I could go to bed. The windows had gaps as much as an inch that let in the weather. Daddy stuffed old fabric, paper, or plastic in the cracks to minimize the cold and dampness. During strong storms, Daddy would take the feather mattress from his and Mama's bed and hold it against the front door to keep it from flying open and letting in the storm. Thunder and wind would shake the whole house causing it to creak and pop so loudly that we feared it would collapse into a pile of wood and children.

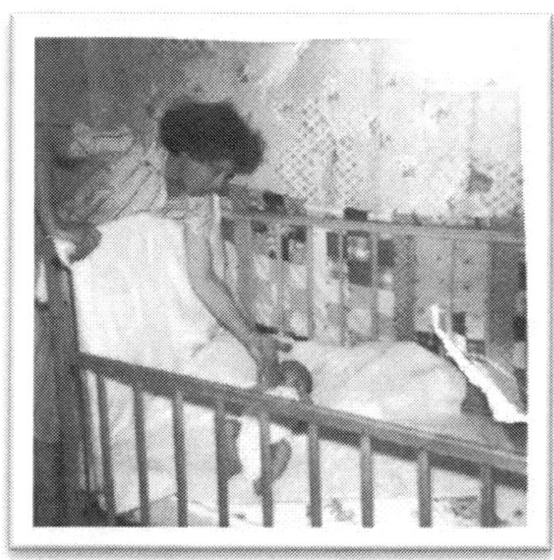

MAMA SOOTHING LINDA TO SLEEP

I recall the remains of linoleum on the floors. The floors were mostly bare wood but scraps from previous years' efforts to add color to the dreary house remained. I remember looking at the patches of flowery linoleum that survived, wondering what it must have looked like before the years of wear turned it into a memory. On the walls, layers and layers of wallpaper peeled off in various stages, revealing dozens of patterns that I studied, deciding which one I liked best on any given day. The ceiling, brown from years of smoke and dotted with even darker circles left by the rain, threatened to cave in with the slightest touch. Many of the exterior asphalt shingles were missing, due partially to children innocently removing them to hear the crackle and feel the rough texture. The front porch was the best. It spanned the whole front of the house, which really did not mean much. It was also the least worn and damaged part of the house, and I remember being proud of our front porch.

MARY, JUNE, VICKIE HOLDING ME &
JANIE HOLDING LINDA

We were not children who had piles of toys. If we were not hiding, paralyzed by fear, we would be running and playing in the yard or on the hills surrounding our tiny piece of ground. We played hide and seek, and 'you're it' our version of tag, Mother May I, and Red Light, Green Light. We played baseball with a tin can for a ball and a stick for a bat. We made tin-can telephones and started digging a hole to China on numerous occasions, though we never quite reached China. Knowing what I know now, it is best we didn't.

When Daddy had an old sheet of plastic left over from work, we dug a hole and covered it with plastic. This was our swimming pool. The well where we got our water was a good distance away so it could take a while to fill a swimming pool. It is difficult to learn to swim in ten gallons of water. We played jacks on the porch, often using small rocks for jacks and played hopscotch in the yard, drawing the blocks by scratching the dirt with a rock. Linda and I would "drive" daddy's car and smoke cigarettes that we made ourselves by collecting small sticks and breaking them into the perfect size to fit into one of mama's or daddy's empty cigarette boxes. We hunted and collected "hicker"nuts and black walnuts and waited for them to dry and then cracked them open on the big rock that was our front step. If we were lucky, Daddy allowed us to use his hammer, if not we could always find a big rock to crack them with. What most people walked by without notice, we cherished as a rare and well-earned treat. Best of all were the swings daddy made by tying a rope to a tree and attaching it to an old tire.

This child's play only occurred on "good days" when Jerry was out on a drinking binge, at work on the rare occasion that he held down a job or was spending the day with his wife and children. If Jerry was at home, we would be safely tucked away, playing far away from him or sitting in one of our hiding places, comforting one another, looking out for one another, praying for one another.

Directly behind and a few yards from our house lived daddy's parents whom we called Maw and Papa. Despite their ~~close~~ proximity, we seldom saw them and rarely were we in their house. This was Mama's doing, not Maw's and Papa's. Mama was forever afraid of imposing on others, and she despised the thought of her children being a nuisance.

Maw was a petite woman, standing no more than five feet tall, but what she lacked in height, she made up for with her astonishingly long hair—at least six feet of it. Every evening, without fail, she would sit carefully working a brush through the long, silken strands before twisting them into a neat bun atop her head. I was mesmerized by the speed at which she completed this task, longing for hair as beautiful and flowing as hers.

There was something gentle about Maw, a quiet presence that made you feel seen without a word needing to be spoken. She had a way of looking at you that made it seem as if she knew what you were thinking. Her gentle kindness wasn't loud or showy; it was subtle, displayed into small gestures—a knowing glance, a soft touch, an unspoken understanding. Maw must have known what went on in our home but was powerless to intervene.

One muggy day, in the peak of summer when the garden vegetables were ready to harvest, Mamma sent me to borrow Maw's canner. I knocked on the door, and when Maw answered, I stood on the porch looking down at my feet as if she could read my mind, (and I'm not sure she couldn't). Maw invited me in. I followed her through the door and sat on the sofa where she pointed. I warned Maw that Mama told me to come right back. She smiled faintly, as if to dismiss Mama's orders. She pulled a kitchen chair over to the refrigerator, grabbed the long skirt of her dress, and stepped up on the chair to reach the canner from where she stored it. She placed it on the kitchen table and told me to go to the fridge and get a doughnut. I declined, saying I was not hungry which Maw knew was not the case. We were not allowed to accept food from anyone outside our home and we were forbidden to open the refrigerator, even at our house. Walking home, I held back tears, grieving the loss of the doughnut and the chance to surprise Linda with such a rare treat. In retrospect, I imagine Mama would have been hurt to know I refused the treat simply to follow her rules.

I often heard my older siblings whisper about some unresolved tension between Mama and Maw. They spoke of an old disagreement or misunderstanding that was left unsettled between them. One sister hinted that Maw may have felt her son had taken on more than she would have liked in his wife and family. But whatever had happened was beyond what my young mind could process. To me, Maw was simply Maw, gentle, quiet and forever brushing her impossibly long hair.

Papa was a gentle man, quiet and cheerful. Papa always had a pleasant and welcoming smile on his face. He often sat on a small chair tilted on its back legs, perched on his front porch or resting under a shaded tree. He predictably could be seen carving a wooden figure for whichever grandchild happened by as he added his finishing touch, or carving bites from the stalk of a head of cabbage Maw had harvested from their garden. Even at the age of five or six, I thought Papa was a handsome man.

MAW AND PAPA

My older sisters, who had more time with Papa, spoke fondly of him, painting a picture of a man full of personality and humor, far more vibrant than the one I recall from my fragmented memories. They had the privilege of truly knowing him, experiencing his presence in a way I never could. I feel cheated somehow that I never sat at Papa's feet as he carved a precious figurine for me. I grieve for the lost time, the possibility of being the light of his life the way my grandchildren are mine. Maw and Papa felt more like Daddy's parents than my grandparents. What a loss to never experience the bond between a child and her grandmother or grandfather.

I clearly remember the day Papa died. He was in the hospital where Daddy visited him daily, always accompanied by one of my sisters. That day as Daddy walked to the car, I noticed he was alone. "Who's going with you, Daddy?" I asked. "No one could make it this time," he said quietly. Even though Daddy and I weren't close then, something inside me couldn't let him go alone. I offered to go with him, and he didn't protest. The drive to the hospital was uncomfortable, leaving me just wishing it would end.

When we reached the hospital. Daddy walked over to Papa's bed, his movements slow and deliberate. Gently, he placed his hand on Papa's leg, a simple touch—one filled with love, grief, and a lifetime of memories. And at that very moment, Papa took his last breath. I stood frozen, my heart aching for Daddy. And though I knew my presence could never take away his pain, I was grateful I was there. At the very least, he wasn't alone.

Next to Maw and Papa's house on Prancy Ridge lived a couple with two daughters. The father, a small man fewer than five feet tall, used crutches due to childhood polio that had partially paralyzed him and stunted his growth. His wife, his faithful and protective caregiver, did heavy lifting around the house. As young girls, their daughters intrigued us. They had an untamed freedom about them, running barefoot through the yard in nothing but their underwear, unbothered by what anyone might think. We often whispered about them when we were out of earshot. We couldn't look away, oddly envious of their carefree defiance, something we didn't fully understand but secretly admired.

The homes at our end of Prancy Ridge were all occupied by family, yet the road saw more traffic than one might expect. The reason was no mystery. Just over the hill stood the home of the local bootlegger, a man who kept the community well supplied with liquor and seemed to know everyone's secrets. Trucks and cars rolled up and down the dirt road at all hours, their drivers avoiding eye contact with us as they passed, as if acknowledging their presence would confirm what everyone already knew. The good thing about having a bootlegger on our dirt road is that he always kept the road in good condition. For us little kids, living out in the sticks, seeing the road grader every few weeks was the peak of excitement.

Daddy, being ever the handyman, built a set of secret compartments for the bootlegger. Local law enforcement surely was aware of our neighbor's service to the community. Daddy got a few bucks or a few bottles for his labor depending on who is telling the story. I never saw Daddy drink more than a beer or two, so I choose to believe he built hiding places for the bootlegger for pure and honest reasons.

Over the hill in front of our house lived Mama's parents. We called them Mom and Dad. Mom was a soft-spoken woman with bobbed raven black hair, while Dad was a tall husky man who always dressed in overalls and smelled of chewing tobacco. I assume we called them Mom and Dad because we did so as children imitating Mama and were just never corrected. Mom used to come and visit Mama once a year in the summer. Dad came often and sat on the kitchen porch stoop and played with us kids.

MOM AND DAD

Mom and dad had six children including three daughters that did not leave home until late in their thirties. The neighbors called them old maids, but I did not understand this as a child as they never cleaned house for us, and I did not ever see them wearing an apron.

One sister, Mary, married young and moved to Georgia with her husband. They had six children including two young boys. They were ~~very~~ close in age and according to their mother they were inseparable. One autumn afternoon, their school organized a fire safety demonstration, complete with the opportunity for all the students to take a ride on a real fire truck. The two boys, as always, took their place side by side on the truck. As the fire truck rounded a curve, it tipped over, crashing onto its side. In an instant, the boys were gone. Mary was also hurt badly as was one of the other children. If I remember correctly, they were unable to attend the boys' funerals. Mary, completely grief stricken became depressed and very soon she and her husband divorced. Unable to find her way through the darkness, she died much too young, leaving behind four other children who had already lost too much. She died alone, her body giving out long before her time.

Behind Mom and Dad's house was a small pond that was home to a bluegill named Cindy. Dad had trained this fish to come to him when he called "her" name. He would start over the hill calling Cindy and you could hear the water splashing. By the time Dad reached the bank, she would be there waiting for him. He would tap on the side an old coffee can that was full of soil and some fishing worms he dug, and she would nearly come out of the water to reach her dinner. The local paper did a story on Dad and Cindy. Dad was so proud that he showed the paper to everyone who came within hearing distance of him. Dad and Cindy were even featured on the local television news interest section.

After Mom died, Mom and Dad's youngest daughter moved out and began doing odd jobs to support her independence. At around age forty, she started a relationship with a man twenty years her junior and had one child. I always thought that having a baby was the reason she pursued a relationship. He was the joy of her life!

PRANCY RIDGE

My earliest memory feels like a black-and-white movie, with Daddy, and Jerry, and me as the main characters. I was about five years old, running out the front door in a panic. I have a hazy memory of my siblings; all of us trying to get out through the door, desperate for someone to hear us and come to help. Inside, there was a fire in the living room, caused by Jerry pulling a burning stick of wood from the stove and setting it on the floor. As I rushed to the door, I heard something crash through the window. The TV and a river of broken glass came flying at me. The TV landed on my foot. But I didn't stop. I just kept running, leaping off the porch as fast as I could. In one last fleeting moment, I turned around to see my daddy's glasses flying off his face and across the room just as Jerry hit him in the jaw with his fist.

That was my introduction to survival, a moment of terror that would become a constant for the next forty years. It marked the beginning of my life with fear—fear that never left and ultimately became a part of me. I didn't experience peace until I was forty-five years old. That's when I started to experience days without fear and nights without nightmares. But for most of my life, the weight of fear consumed me, creating in me a constant battle to keep from going under.

Life was predictable on Prancy Ridge. We relished the much-needed calm and quiet, but the lingering isolation wore on both the children and adults. Mama and Daddy never had a telephone except for the two years that Jerry was in Vietnam. A phone was an extravagance that didn't belong in a house where shoes were shared, dinners were missed, and every penny was spent before it was made. Communication with the outside world was limited to word of mouth and a black and white TV. We were able to watch cartoons for an hour or two after school and on Saturday. Cartoons were such a treat for us. A knock at the door brought with it a sense of excitement, a pleasant and mysterious anticipation. These occurrences were few and far between.

One older gentleman would visit occasionally. His name was Owen. He had a smile that stretched from one ear to the other and he loved to make us children laugh. My sisters say he drank with Daddy, but I don't recall that. I clearly remember, though, that Owen had a peg leg. His leg was genuinely made of a stick of wood with a flat wooden bottom, no foot to deaden the sound as he danced across the floor. And he did dance, to the delight of the children and even Mama, who was not big on nonsense. I do not recall how he lost his leg but as a child, I was endlessly fascinated by the way he moved and the hollow sound of his step against the floor.

Owen's visits, though infrequent, were always special. Every so often, he would slip us kids a shiny quarter, a small yet thrilling gift. The moment that coin touched our hands, we could hardly wait for our older sisters to make the half-mile trek to the marina store where they would carefully choose candy to bring back for us. Those sweet treats, though rare, felt like the greatest of luxuries. When I think of Owen now, the vivid memory of that simple joy—unwrapping a piece of candy, and letting the sugary taste linger brings a smile to my face.

Occasionally, another group of visitors, who brought both excitement and unease, would stop by our house. A band of gypsies would arrive in a creaky, old, covered wagon that looked like it had seen better days. Their coffee pot and cookware hung off the sides, clanging and rattling as the wagon made its way up the hill. The sound was unmistakable, and you would hear the clanging long before you saw the wagon. That wagon seemed like something out of a storybook, but it was real life, and in my young mind, it was fascinating.

Mama, however, was not so charmed by the arrival of the gypsies. The second she heard the wagon rattling; she would round up all the young ones and herd us inside the same way she would herd in her hens when she planned to have one for dinner. The clanging of the pans was more like a fire or tornado alarm to her. "Get inside!" she would holler. "Lock the door!" She was convinced by the local rumors that they only came around in hopes of stealing little girls.

Even as a young child, I did not believe this rumor and I certainly didn't worry about them stealing any of us. Instead, I saw no reason to hide from them and I would sneak to the window and watch through the curtains, just to catch a glimpse of them. To me, they were exciting and mysterious, nothing like anyone else I had ever seen. They always seemed to carry an air of drama about them, particularly the mother. She had long, dark hair that shimmered in the sunlight, falling loose down the middle of her back. Her long skirt touched the ground as she walked, depending on the weather, a ring of dust, dirt, or mud accumulated on the bottom of her skirt as proof. She tended to keep one hand resting on her stomach. Mama said it made it easier to snatch up little girls who wandered by, but I thought it made her look stern, a force to be reckoned with and I admired her for that. It was apparent that she was the one in charge.

Accompanying her were two preteen boys who walked around with their thumbs in their suspenders. I thought it made them seem older than their years and too purposeful for young boys. At times, a mysterious teenage girl was with them. She mostly stayed in the wagon but occasionally walked holding the boys' hands. She was also very stoic but occasionally would show a hint of a smile. She was, like her mother, tall and slim with long raven black hair. My older sisters told me the gypsies came by because Mama sold candy, and she would barter with them, trading candy for whatever she needed from their wagon. I did not know the details of the trades, but I remember the strange sense of excitement that filled the air when the wagon rolled up. There was always something mesmerizing about their visits. The gypsies would linger near the house, their voices carrying so that if I squeezed my ear tightly against the window, I could hear bits and pieces of the conversation. Straining to hear, I couldn't tell whether they asked any questions about the little girls locked in the house. I never saw them do anything untoward, but Mama's suspicion would not waver. Those visits were like something out of a dream, a slice of a world far removed from our quiet little lives.

Many times, one of us children would wake up on a winter morning with a harsh, barking cough caused by a viral infection called croup. It was terrifying for a child to struggle for each breath as the condition tightened the airways, leaving us gasping and anxious. It was terrifying for Mama too. Mama, always resourceful, and trying not to show fear over illness or injury, quickly went to work to calm her frightened child. She had her own remedy for the croup. She would warm a piece of cornbread left over from a previous meal and brew a strong cup of coffee. She believed the rough texture of the cornbread helped clear the throat and the warmth of the coffee loosened the congestion in the airway, soothed our nerves, and gave us comfort. The scent of the coffee seemed to calm us even before we took a sip.

We would sit at the kitchen table together, taking small bites of cornbread, listening to the calming sound of Mama's voice, assuring us everything would be okay. Though we never fully understood the science behind it, there was something deeply reassuring about the ritual. It always seemed to help, if only in making us feel cared for, comforted, and less afraid in those anxious moments. It was a small act, but it made the world feel a little safer.

Growing up, I was often teased at school. I would show up in clothes that had not been washed because doing laundry was not always an option. In the summer, our well would run dry, and there was no money for the laundromat. Mama did what she could, but it was not enough to keep us from standing out. Other kids called me "white trash," though I did not really know what it meant at the time, so I ignored it. The comments about how I smelled or might have lice hit harder. Unfortunately, they were not wrong. Baths and clean clothes were not always possible, and it showed, making me an easy target for their jokes. Kids would wrinkle their noses and move away, whispering or laughing behind my back. Their cruelty was not subtle, and every glance or word just reminded me of how much I stood out.

I remember trying to hold my head high, even though I felt small inside. Mama apologized, saying she was doing the best she could, I could see the weight of it on her face. The laughter still echoes in my mind, a reminder of those bleak and lonely days.

MY SWEET MAMA

My mama taught us three things consistently and with conviction: do not make fun of people, do not steal, and do not say or do anything to upset our brother. The third was not spoken, but it was cut into our brains as surely as if she had taken a knife and dug the entire length of the blade into our young flesh. Lying wasn't harped on so much but we did not want to get caught in a lie. We listened to Mama and Daddy. We were good children.

I loved my mama immensely. She did not hand out strong discipline indiscriminately. We suffered the occasional punishment that could spin a person's head around and leave whelps on little legs. These generally flew out of nowhere when she lost her temper over too much noise, too much work, or too much worry that just caused her to lose control. When mama did strike out at you, she put the fear of God in you.

But mama was mostly quiet, occupied with the many duties that called her away from her children every day. Mama didn't have time to spend with her children. She spent every minute of the day working at one thing or another to make our lives better. I do not recall mama ever playing around, reading, or even sitting outside with us as we played in the yard. Mama was not affectionate. She never kissed or hugged us; never told us she loved us. But she did love us, and we knew it. This all changed after Jerry went to prison. Mama never let us leave the house without saying "I love you, be good and be careful."

Mama did not have much down time. Although we never had new clothes from a department store, we did get new clothes during the months that daddy could work. Mama had a sewing machine in her bedroom and every day after school, Linda and I raced off the bus into Mama's room to see what she had made for us that day. We often had a new outfit waiting for us. The other kids started to notice our new clothes and some had the nerve to ask us where we got them. "My mama made it." I would proudly say. Most of them did not believe me and just walked away. Some continued to ask and began to complement us on what we wore. One parent asked Mama to make a prom dress for her daughter. Mama declined because she said she had to make two dresses for her own girls. We were surprised that we were going to the junior prom, and that our mother was going to make our dresses. And did she? I still remember my red and pink prom dress with the see-through sleeves. It was beautiful and I was proud to wear it. Linda had the same dress in green. It was nearly as pretty as mine.

Mama worked hard to raise us to be obedient, compassionate, and kind. She lived with evil her entire life, so she taught us to be good and do good, and I believe every one of us has strived to be good and do good. We loved and respected our parents too much to be anything else.

Daddy was the opposite. He liked to make toys for his children. He taught us to ride bikes that he put together from scraps he would find here and there, usually at the dump. He would tell us bedtime stories until we fell asleep. Daddy was affectionate. For me, he was overly affectionate. Affection made me uncomfortable, and this caused me to avoid him more and more as I grew older.

One thing I loved most about Daddy was his playing the guitar. He used to rock me to sleep by shaking the bed as he played his guitar and sang. “The Wildwood Flower”. I still love that song and hearing it brings me joy and great peace. What I wouldn’t give to hear Daddy play “The Wildwood Flower” again.

Daddy was a self-taught guitar player as were all my brothers. It seemed to be in their blood. Watching them play made it seem effortless, like the music just lived in their fingertips. I have always yearned to play like Daddy and my brothers but have found it incredibly difficult. Still the desire hasn't left me. A dear friend of mine who knew how much learning to play meant to me, hand delivered a guitar to my door. That gesture moved me more than words could say. My bucket list contains three items. The first was to meet Tom Petty. The last is to go wild boar hunting and right in the middle, still waiting to be fulfilled, is learning to play the guitar like daddy did, with heart and soul.

Daddy was often away for long stretches and there were times when he didn't have a car to get to work. During these times he hitchhiked sometimes covering distances of more than 100 miles just to get to his job. He would be gone all week and then hitchhike back on weekends. When daddy was away, I remained in a constant state of worry. Whenever I got a cut or a scratch, something in my eye, or any minor ailment, I would always look for Daddy. I just needed to hear him tell me it was ok. That was all I needed for reassurance. Mama could say the same thing, but somehow it never felt right unless it came from Daddy. His calm response and competent manner made it feel like everything would be just fine. I also had this quiet fear that one day something might happen to me and daddy wouldn't be there to fix it or tell me everything would be all right. That thought always lingered in the back of my mind even if I tried not to dwell on it. Daddy often brought us a treat home, usually Cracker Jacks which was my favorite treat then and still is. He would sometimes get out of the car with a watermelon, the greatest treat of all!

Sundays were bad days at our house. Mama would often cry on Sunday as Daddy was leaving, which ended in most of us crying too. It always surprised me when Mama was sad to see Daddy go because she seldom showed Daddy any affection. It never occurred to me that she cared for him.

Water was something we never took for granted. We had a three-gallon galvanized bucket with a handle and a galvanized dipper that served as our faucet. Instead of grabbing a glass from the cabinet and pouring water from a sink, we would take the dipper and drink straight from it then put it back in the bucket. Everyone in the family used the same dipper throughout the day. We did not own a set of glasses and just enough coffee cups for the adults who drank coffee.

To fill the bucket, we made the thirty or so yard trek over the hill to the deep well. We dropped a bucket attached to a string into the well letting it fall twenty feet to reach the water and waited for it to tip over and fill.

Then we pulled it back up by the string. Mama always tied a fishing sinker onto the handle to keep the bucket from just floating on top of the water. Instead of a sink, Mama placed a small table in the corner of the kitchen where she kept an aluminum pan for washing dishes. A similar table with a smaller pan was kept near the back door for washing our hands as we came in from playing or after using the outside toilet.

For laundry, she used an old-fashioned wringer washer that we filled with water carried from the well in three-gallon buckets and heated on the cook stove. It took us children several trips over the hill to fill the washer and the rinsing tub with water.

Mama and Daddy had a fake mantle in their bedroom. It was off limits to us children as that was where mama kept her purse and Daddy kept his wallet and most guarded of all, the family Bible rested there. Oddly enough, we were not allowed to touch the Bible because it was so precious and not to be used as a plaything. I loved sneaking into Mama's room when Daddy was at work and Mama was in the garden. She was good for three or more hours away when she was in the garden. Crawling into the middle of their bed, I could flip through the pages all afternoon. I was too young to read, but I could spend hours studying the pictures. I always kept an ear out for Mama's soft footsteps.

Mama would often cut her hands as she would not touch gloves while working in the garden. She wanted to feel the soil. This happened to be one of those days when her hands slipped on a blade of grass she was pulling and left a small bleeding slice in all four fingers. She came inside for a bandage that she kept in her purse. The door gently opened, and I died for six seconds. Mama's voice miraculously brought me back to life. "Tammy, you know you are not supposed to be in here. I know Mama, I just wanted to read the Bible." "But you can't read", Mama said. "I'm looking at the pictures and pretending." She decided that was a good enough reason to be in her room.

Poor Mama. I felt so bad for lying to her I was not on a holy mission. I was flipping through the pages, stopping at every page that contained illustrations. I was looking for the pictures with naked men and women. I never, even as a grown woman had the courage to tell her what a sinner her preschool daughter was.

It took me two years to gain the courage to sneak into Mama's room again. And this time it was a royal screw-up. One morning, I woke up and decided I did not want to go to school. You didn't miss school in my house unless you were bleeding, throwing up in the moment, or had a fever that could catch the sheets on fire. Not that school was that important to my family, but Mama's sanity was. She wanted us to learn. (To get out of the damned house.) I tried making myself throw up, cutting my ear off was not out of the question but it was going to be the last resort. I could do a fever....so easily. I went into Mama's bedroom, opened her purse, and grabbed the thermometer. I tried holding it under my tongue. You never know. I then held it under my arm for at least five minutes thinking this was the trick to heat it up and show a fever that would make Mama pass out. Not registering in my young mind, it was only going to get as warm as my underarm.

It suddenly occurred to me, a sure-fire way to register a fever on the thermometer. I went out into the living room and quickly snatched up daddy's cigarette lighter. I hid it under my blouse and hurried back to the bedroom. With my little hands, it took several tries to get the lighter to ignite. When it did, I held it up to the silver end of the thermometer, thinking it would take a good while for it to become warm enough to convince mama that I was sick enough to stay home from school.

Much to my horror, as soon as the flame came into contact with the thermometer the end popped off and the mercury fell to the bed in perfect little balls. My mind raced. My heart pounded. I reached down with my trembling hands, picked up the mercury, ran outside, and tossed it into the grass. All the time wondering if a heart attack would get me excused from school for a day. I got dressed and went out to catch the bus.

The next time I woke up determined I did not want to go to school I had a much better plan in place. I got dressed, stood out by the bus stop which for us was a huge maple tree with a trunk about four feet wide. I waited with Linda and Jeff for the bus to come, never telling them my plan for fear that they would rat me out. The bus finally came. I heard the door creak open and stood against that tree like a statue hoping the driver would not see me and honk that dreadful horn. I watched as Jeff and Linda boarded the bus and waved goodbye to them, head down, fingers barely moving. They both just smiled sweetly at me and waved goodbye probably knowing they would never see me again. As the bus drove away, I felt a sense of relief. That was short lived as I realized I was not home free yet.

I stood behind the tree until about 10 o'clock, a good two hours when I finally got up the nerve to go into the house. As I approached the porch, I saw Mama standing right in the doorway. Once I recovered from the terror of seeing her there, it registered that she had her back to the porch and to me. She was ironing. I took a deep breath and continued toward her trying to muster up the courage and find the words to confess my sin. "What are you doing here?" Mama's voice soft and comforting as she turned toward me. I wanted to run to her and tell her how sorry I was, but I had been thoroughly trained to stifle such nonsense. Barely holding back the tears, I answered "I didn't get on the bus, Mama." She quickly turned around back to the ironing board. I did not know why at the time, but I know why now. She could not let me see her laughing at my sad response. She looked toward the couch and said "Go get a quilt and lay down, you'll feel better in a little bit and Robert can take you to school.

I didn't want to go to school late, but I wasn't going to let that thought steal my victory. Even if it was just briefly, the relief and the comfort of resting on the couch under a quilt at home alone with mama was as close to Heaven as I needed to be that day. She was right, I did feel better. I could have stayed there forever in the bright light of the living room, a cool breeze blowing through the open door, and mama all to myself.

When us children gave Mama and Daddy trouble at bedtime, Daddy had a special bedtime story he would tell us. It was called "Hang Down Billy". The story was about a fellow who lived in our attic. He stayed put and was nothing to be afraid of unless Daddy had to call on him. In that case, Daddy would yell into our room and tell us if we did not settle down, he was going to call Hang Down Billy. This was generally all it took to seal our lips. If it didn't, daddy would begin his ritual. 'Billy, oh Billy, hang down one leg Billy." We weren't too afraid of Daddy, so sometimes this made us laugh resulting in, “Hang down another leg Billy”. Sometimes Daddy would get as far as asking Billy to hang down one arm but that is about as far as it ever went. Funny or not, we did not want to meet Billy face to face. And we never did. When we were older and hang down Billy didn't do the trick, Daddy would sic Raw Hide and Bloody Bones on us. I wonder if Billy is still in the attic listening for the final call to hang down his head. And if old Raw Hide is still under the porch waiting for daddy to open the door and let him in; or did they fade into nowhere the day that fear was replaced with forgiveness.

Jerry thrilled in the game he invented that Linda, and I later called the broomstick game. Jerry was getting ready for work. Linda and I were playing together, and Mama told us we were making too much noise. She probably said it to avoid upsetting Jerry, as mornings were especially volatile, in his presence. We carried on, paying little attention to Mama’s warning. Then suddenly, I was yanked up by the neck of my shirt. “Did you hear what Mama said? You need to learn to listen—and I know how to teach you. He left the room, returning quickly with a broom and a mop. I felt a wave of relief. “He’s just going to make us clean.” I thought. I had imagined something far worse when he walked out. He put the broom and mop on the floor and told us to kneel on them. He warned us that if we did not stay in that position all day, the punishment would be much worse when he returned home from work. He informed us that he would know by looking at our knees whether we did as he said.

Once he was out of the driveway, Mama told us to get up. I was disappointed that Mama was willing to defy him when he was gone, but not willing to defend us against him when he was in the act of hurting us. As the day went on, Linda and I played in the house while Mama sewed. As the evening rolled around, Mama called us into the living room and told us to get back on our knees. It would not be long before Jerry was home and if he didn't see marks on our knees, it could be really bad. Jerry came in through the door and looked over at us, his face expressionless. "Stand-up" he ordered. He inspected our legs and then without any sign of emotion, he walked away muttering, "You can go".

It was Sunday morning, and it was my turn. Linda and I could not both go to church every week. We alternated because we only had one pair of shoes nice enough to wear to God's house. This Sunday was extra special, and I knew I would make Him proud. A box of donated clothes from a neighbor had arrived earlier in the week and inside was a little yellow sweater with pearly white buttons. The sweater was warm and soft, and as soon as I slipped it on. I made up my mind. It was mine, and mine alone.

Throughout Mass, my hands moved up and down the buttons like I was strumming a guitar as I had seen Daddy do so many times. I could almost hear the music drowning out the words I had come to hear. I knew it was wrong, a selfish indulgence that left a black mark on my soul, but as hard as I tried, my mind kept wandering. On the way home, all I could think about was how to keep the sweater for myself and make sure Linda never got a chance to wear it.

As we pulled into the driveway, an idea popped into my head. Our porch was underpinned with concrete blocks, and I remembered one of them was slightly displaced, creating a small gap. Nervously, I waited for everyone to go inside, then made my way to the porch. I knelt in the gravel and dirt, ignoring the sharp rocks pressing into my knees through my white church leotards. I slipped off the sweater, tears streaming down my face as I whispered a prayer for forgiveness. I added a desperate plea for my secret to remain safe forever. Then, with trembling hands, I shoved the sweater behind the block. It was difficult to move, especially for a frail little girl but I managed to push the block tightly back into place. My hands scraped against the rough concrete, leaving tiny cuts on my palms. When I finally gave it one last shove, my knees slid painfully backward on the gravel, tearing through the fabric of my leotards and into the skin. Losing my balance, I fell forward, my chin striking the block's edge. Blood began dripping from my chin, my scraped hands, and my knees.

Panicked, I ran inside, silently praying not to run into Mama. But I must not have prayed hard enough because as soon as I opened the door, there she was, mama and me face-to-face. Mama did not panic at the sight of blood. After raising eleven kids, it hardly fazed her anymore. She asked calmly, "What happened?" I lied, telling her I tripped while running up the steps to the porch. She accepted my answer without question and told me to go wash up with soap and water. She did not even scold me for ruining my church leotards, probably because the dirt, tears, and blood streaked across my face told her I had had enough grief for one day.

I never wore that little yellow sweater again, but neither did Linda; and that was my goal. It was not about her. I loved my little sister. I just wanted something that was mine and mine alone. That night, as I lay in bed, I whispered my usual prayers and added ten Our Fathers, three Hail Mary's, and the Act of Contrition, imagining that those prayers were likely what Father would assign me if I ever had the courage to tell him about my sin in the confessional. I cried myself to sleep as I thought about lying to Mama.

That little yellow sweater caused me a lot of grief, but for a few hours, it gave me something precious. It made a little girl who never doubted being ugly, feel pretty. For just a minute, it let me imagine what it must be like to have a closet full of clean, pretty clothes, a warm comfy bed to sleep in, and a cupboard full of scrumptious snacks.

By the time I was seven, I already knew without a doubt who I would marry. It had little to do with his looks and more to do with his talent. My husband would one day without a doubt be Buck Owens. Mama was not happy about this. She had quite a disdain for Buck Owens, both his looks and his talents. Mama used to have us girls rub her feet and pop her toes after she had worked in the garden all day. When I would pop her toes if her pinky toe popped then I would tease her and tell her she had to marry Buck Owens. Of course, we both knew this was nothing more than a joke, because he was destined for me. I loved his voice, and I loved his songs, and I really did not think he was bad looking. Most of all I loved the way he played guitar.

I still love Buck Owens. I still love his songs. I still do not think he is too bad looking and I still love the way he plays guitar, but I chose another to be my husband, and I have to say I do not regret that.

The other love of my life at that time was Johnny Cash. I thought he was the most beautiful thing I ever laid my eyes on. I never heard a Johnny Cash song that did not make me happy. My very favorite was "I Walk the Line". It was not just my favorite Johnny Cash song; it was my very favorite song. I promised myself that when I grew up that I would dance to "I Walk the Line" at my wedding. Thinking back. I am not sure what Buck Owens would have thought of that.

Daily life on Prancy Ridge was built on necessity and predictability. Outside on the back porch, Mama kept her "hippen bucket". It held three to four gallons of water and when full, it was very painful to carry due to the narrow handle digging into the palm of our hand. This tool was primarily used for washing the babies' dirty cloth diapers, which Mama referred to as "hippens." This was done daily due to the limited supply of diapers and having at least two children in diapers most of the time. The dirty diapers were just thrown in the bucket, poop and all, so washing them by hand in cold water was a stinky, nasty job. You could not wash the stink off your hands, and the stench would last all day.

As the diapers wore thin with use, Mama repurposed the old cloths by folding and layering them to serve as feminine protection. She would wash and hang them on the clothesline to dry and reuse them repeatedly. This was one more bit of evidence proving Mama's ability to make do with limited resources. Every scrap of worn cloth found a purpose in her hands. Looking back, I am struck by how much quiet strength and determination she poured into even the most menial tasks. Remarkably, this was one chore she never asked me to assist with, leaving me both grateful and in awe of her self-sufficiency.

Mama always waited eagerly for daddy to get home from work on Friday. By then the cupboard was bare, and she was barely able to scrape up a simple supper or more likely, we had no supper at all until they got home from the store. On one such trip, Jerry insisted on driving them. He was in a kind of sour mood, but he usually was, and if he wasn't, it was just a matter of time. They headed to the grocery store, Mama and Jerry in the front seat and daddy in the back. It was a considerable distance to town, and we never expected them back for at least two hours.

It was long past that and we began to worry. A car pulled into the driveway, and we ran out thinking it was Mama and Daddy but instead it was one of our neighbors. She was there to deliver the news that Mama, Daddy, and Jerry had been in a car accident and Daddy had been taken to the hospital in Louisville. The neighbor told us that Mama and Jerry would be home soon and that she had come to drive one of us to stay with daddy in Louisville.

We later found out how the accident happened. On the way home, Daddy and Jerry got into an argument. Jerry began driving recklessly and lost control of the car. He tried to round a curve at a high speed and ran through a fence. Jerry came out without a scratch, but Daddy sustained a broken back and was rushed to Louisville to undergo back surgery. He remained in the hospital for two weeks and returned home in a back brace that he wore for several weeks. Mama suffered multiple injuries in the accident, including several broken ribs, multiple cuts and bruises, and a miscarriage. I vaguely recall Jerry and Mama pulling into the driveway, and Mama getting out of the car with a bandage covering her head. It is heartbreaking to think of the fear that Mama and Daddy felt that day and the physical pain they endured.

While daddy was still wearing the back brace, Jerry, in a fit of rage stormed into Mama and Daddy's room and got Daddy's rifle. He came back into the living room where all us children played, waving and pointing it wildly throughout the room. Mama froze and Daddy stood ready, staring at the barrel of the rifle. When it was within reach, Daddy grabbed the barrel and wrestled the rifle out of Jerry's grip, slammed it into the floor, and broke the stock off completely, which rendered the rifle unusable. In the process, Daddy reinjured his back adding to his recovery time and delaying once again his ability to earn a badly needed paycheck.

Not long after, Jerry was driving daddy's car when he got into another accident, leaving the body dented and twisted. Instead of focusing on making it right with Daddy, Jerry set out to find the highest estimates he could. When the insurance check arrived, he decided that since he was the reason the money was coming in, he had the right to keep it, and he did.

Daddy didn't say much. He rarely did when it came to Jerry, but I could tell he was disappointed that the car looked like hell. But it still ran, and in our world that was good enough. It was just one more example of how things worked in our house. Damage happened. Somebody got paid and we all kept going. If there was a way, Jerry would cause everything that happened to our family, whether good or bad, to tilt in his favor.

Playing outside one day, digging in the dirt with one of Mama's serving spoons with the goal of scratching up enough dirt for dirt cakes, I found a small doll buried in the ground. She had a disproportioned head and short curly blonde hair that was matted together with mud. I continued to dig until she was uncovered enough to pull her from her grave. I took the doll inside and put it in the small aluminum pan where we washed our hands. I set about cleaning her up. I worked on her for a long time, cleaning in between her little toes and making sure that her matted hair was spotless. I brushed her hair until it was just the way I thought it looked when she was new. When I finished cleaning, I dried her off and wrapped a washcloth around her to keep her warm.

I ran into the living room to show Mama what I had found. Jerry was sitting close by in a chair. He immediately grabbed the doll from my hand and with mock shock he asked "Do you know what this is? This is a doll with a big head. Do you know that there are real people who have big heads and people buy these dolls just to make fun of them?" Well, I knew I would never make fun of anybody, and I certainly would not make fun of my doll. I was going to take good care of her.

Jerry took my doll's little blanket off that I had so carefully wrapped her in so he could get a good look at her. At the same time, he opened the stove door. He held her inside the door and asked me what I thought it felt like for her to be that close to the fire. I was not about to answer. The instant he finished the sentence, he let go of her. I watched in quiet horror as she fell into the flame. I could see from where I was standing as the hair that I had so carefully and lovingly cleaned slowly burned off her head. Mama never looked up from what she was doing. I'm sure she knew that if she said anything that the episode would only continue to escalate.

It was picture day at school, and Mama did something out of the ordinary. She parted my hair on the side and clipped in a small yellow duck-shaped barrette. She had picked it up while buying fabric, in anticipation of picture day. At first, I felt uneasy. I had never styled my hair differently before, and worried it might draw too much attention to me. But when I looked in the mirror, I changed my mind. I felt proud wearing it to school.

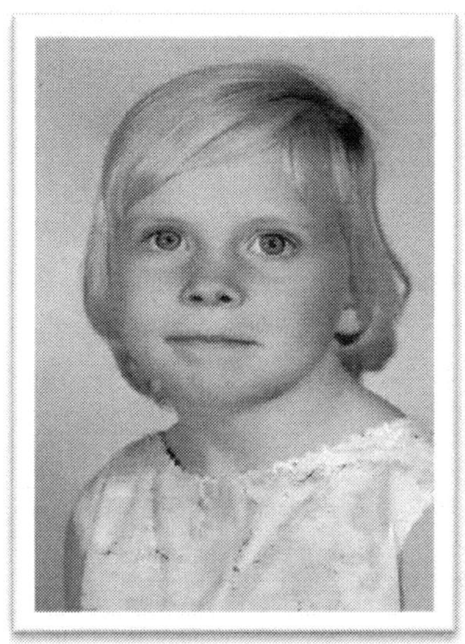

PICTURE DAY

A few weeks later, the pictures arrived. I carried the proof around all day, eager to show Mama. As soon as I got off the bus, I ran into the living room, where she was snapping green beans. I handed her the photo with a big smile, and she smiled back softly. But before I could savor the moment, Jerry snatched the picture from my hand. He held it up, looked at it, and started laughing. "Why do you have mustard in your hair?" he teased. "I bet all the kids at school were laughing at you and calling you Mustard Girl!" My stomach churned as I imagined their taunts and I dreaded going back to school the next day. Before I could react, Jerry held the picture high above his head and began to slowly wrinkle it into a tight ball. “You don’t want anyone seeing that.” he muttered.

Mama didn’t usually buy school pictures. It was not a priority when she had so many mouths to feed and children to care for. But that year she bought the photos. She framed a five-by-seven of the photo and hung it on the wall. I still have that picture. A little blonde-haired girl, her lips barely smiling, her eyes filled with hope. And nestled in her neatly parted hair, a yellow barrette in the shape of a duckling. As seen by an adult me, it is an image that is undeniably beautiful.

Jerry took every opportunity to remind Mama of Larry’s death, digging deeply into her wounds. But one day, it was my turn. Jerry called me into the living room, his voice dark and cold. He demanded that I go into his bedroom to fetch something for him. The room was pitch-black, and I could not turn the light on because we had pull chains instead of wall switches. I was not tall enough to reach the chain. I nervously entered his room, which I was forbidden to enter regularly. He gave me instructions to reach up high, to the top shelf of the closet. and get something. I stretched as far as I could on tiptoe, but nothing was there.

“Can’t you feel anything?” he shouted from the living room. I answered no, but he insisted, “Reach a little further. Way back in the corner. When you get all the way back to the corner, you will find a little bitty head. That is Larry’s head, and it has been there for a long time. Grab it by the hair and bring it to me.” I was terrified, my hands trembling as I reached into the dark space. I had no idea what I would find but I did not dare defy him. Nothing could be as scary as the thought of his anger. My heart raced as I prepared for what I might find in that darkness. “Do you feel it” He asked. “No.”, I timidly replied. After a long pause, he laughed while saying, “Well, I guess he came back to get it and he’s probably still in the closet”. I waited, afraid to move but wanting to run out of the room. But I waited for him to give me permission to go back to the safety of the lighted living room. Every time I passed one of our closets after that I wondered if Larry was still there.

CHARMING CHATTY

In 1969, something miraculous happened. Daddy came to us one day and told us we were moving to a new house. We were overjoyed and had no idea what to expect. He and mom had found a rental house sitting on a cattle farm not far from where we attended school. We were mesmerized by the size of the house which~~, in reality~~, was not much larger than the house we had left. But it was full of light. Light everywhere and the biggest porch we ever saw. Best of all was the shed. When we explored the shed it was filled with abandoned toys. One doll was especially unique. She had an inscription on the back of her neck, “Charming Chatty”. She had a string on her back that when pulled caused the doll to speak, or in this case, creak because the device inside was broken. We didn't mind. We loved and played with her all the same.

One night, we were sleeping in our bed, June, Linda, Mary, and me. Suddenly, out of the darkness, we heard a blood curdling scream. The four of us jumped up to find Charming Chatty standing at the side of our bed nearly touching June’s face and screaming. We were all terrified, but June was especially traumatized as she could not get away from the horror. Without warning, Jerry raised up from the side of the bed where he was hiding and holding the doll. This was even more terrifying. The doll was frightening but not as frightening as having Jerry in our room at night. We never played with her again but Charming Chatty often visited us when were in a deep sleep and each time the results were the same, terrified children and a delighted Jerry.

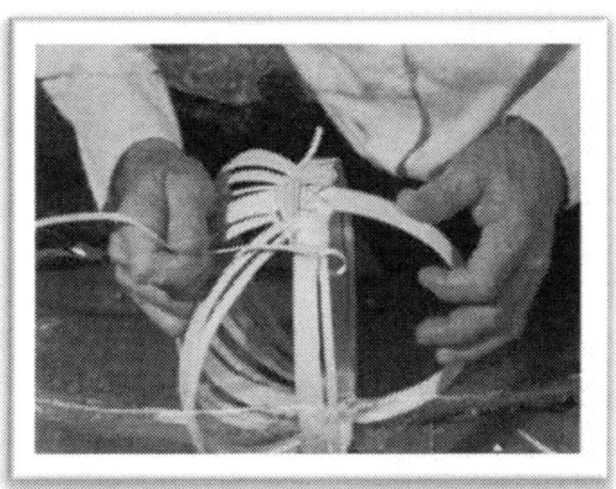

DADDY WORKING ON ONE OF HIS HANDMADE BASKETS

Winters were the lean months for us because daddy was laid off from his construction job. He and Mama made baskets that they sold to a local merchant. These were not the handmade baskets that you buy online or from a mail company and put together. Daddy went out into the woods and hunted for young maple and oak saplings, which were the perfect species and the perfect size for making baskets. He cut them down and carried them back to the house where he quartered them and then took them inside. He and Mama then quartered them again and debarked them followed by carving off thin slices of the quartered pieces. The small slices would be placed on their leg which was protected by a piece of thick denim and then shaped into the 'splits:' by shaving them to a paper-thin piece resembling a ribbon. The next step was to cut a thicker slice from the quarters, sharpening the ends and leaving a wide flat middle. These would be the "ribs". Finally, the frame was constructed by two long thick pieces that would be shaped into a circle and held together by one of the splits. Each end of the ribs would be placed in the frame, ultimately forming a bowl like structure with a handle. Finally, the splits were woven through the ribs to create a truly handmade basket.

Mama and Daddy taught a class on basket making for a short time and daddy developed and published an instructional pamphlet on basket making. Their baskets were featured in some lady's magazines and were spotted by Governor John Y. Brown and Phyllis George Brown which led to an opportunity for him to make custom baskets lined with silk or velvet for Tiffany's and Bloomingdale's to display their lingerie.

DADDY WITH FORMER KY GOVERNOR JOHN Y. BROWN AND HIS WIFE PHYLLIS GEORGE BROWN

Daddy also made baseball caps, baby bassinettes, lamps, and cake holders using the same technique he used to make the baskets. He also made functional pocketknives and guitars.

When we were young, it was not unusual for us to get intestinal worms. Mama always knew when we had them, as she would find them in our stool. Sometimes they were so bad they made us nauseous, and we would struggle to keep any food or water in our stomachs. ~~I would go to the bathroom and use a piece of newspaper for toilet paper, only to pull out long, wriggling worms.~~ One day, at school, I started feeling that familiar nausea. I ran to the bathroom and began throwing up.

After a few rounds of vomiting, I felt weaker and weaker. These were not small, harmless worms; they were long and thin, like fishing worms, twisting inside me. It was terrifying and felt like something I could not escape, like being trapped in my own body. This memory haunts me, as I think of the helplessness of it all. Mama had a home remedy for this ailment too. She would mix sugar with castor oil. The sugar was supposed to make the castor oil more tolerable. Soon up would come everything in our stomach. This was just a band aid, and a miserable one but it beat the alternative.

Mama and Daddy had a huge garden every year, and whatever they grew, Mama found a way to preserve it. She froze vegetables, canned them, or stored them in the cool, dark cellar for the winter months. Their garden was no small affair. It stretched across a half-acre at least, and was filled with row upon row of corn, tomatoes, green beans, potatoes, and dozens of other vegetables. We kids had our own job to do. Armed with a bucket of water and a dipper, we followed along behind Mama and Daddy, carefully watering each plant before covering it with soil. Daddy wasn't the ordinary gardener. He was creative and loved experimenting with different crops.

While he grew the usual staples like tomatoes and green beans, he also filled the garden with heirloom tomatoes, their rich colors ranging from deep purple and pink to bright yellow. These weren't just beautiful; they were sweet, meaty, and bursting with flavor. He planted asparagus and Brussels sprouts, something few neighbors grew. Sometimes, he even grew popcorn, which was a novelty for us kids. Some years, he dedicated a whole section of the land to watermelon and cantaloupes, and when they ripened in the hot summer sun, there was nothing sweeter than cracking one open right there in the field. The garden was more than just food. It was a way of life, a labor of love that fed our family through the seasons.

Daddy's brother and his wife lived on a large farm. A section of the farm was covered in wild blackberries. On weekend mornings, our family would get ready for a day of picking. We dressed from head to toe, making sure our arms and legs were completely covered. After slathering a thick layer of lard on our ankles and wrists to keep the chiggers from burrowing into our skin, we pulled our socks up over our pant legs as an extra precaution. The work was tedious, our hands and arms scratched by thorns, but the reward was worth it. I loved blackberries then and I still do. Every night when I came in from running around, which usually meant hanging out with my friends in the parking lot of one of the grocery stores in town, I would sneak into Mama's closet, dig around until I found a jar, and eat the whole contents, which was one quart. I was fortunate in the fact that most of the family didn't like the seeds in the blackberries. That left plenty of jars for me to enjoy when I came home at night.

In early spring, we hunted mushrooms, scouring the woods and fields for morels. Sometimes, Daddy dried them so we could enjoy their rich flavor later in the year. We also foraged for all kinds of wild greens, our favorite being poke. It was a large plant, growing tall and thick, so it was always plentiful. To prepare it, we stripped the leaves, boiled them in water, then fried them up just like spinach. The stalk, which could grow two to three feet tall and as thick as a quarter, was edible too. Mama chopped it into pieces, coated it in cornmeal, and fried it until it was brown and crispy. She also picked lambs quarter, a tender, wild green, and when the turnips were all harvested, she left the plants to produce turnip greens.

Daddy slaughtered and processed his own hogs occasionally. I remember one time when I was probably three or four years old, I was walking out the front door when suddenly, in through the same door, came a hog weighing about 150 pounds. He missed me but just about an inch. This just about caused my daddy to have a heart attack.

We had plenty to eat in the summertime. In winter when all the vegetables Mama had preserved were gone. food became scarce. "I remember going to Mom and saying I was hungry. She didn't even look up—just said there was nothing to eat." How excruciating that must have been for her.

We had little idea about what the outside world had to offer, and it was probably best that I was so naïve. Still, I always felt a sense of yearning for more. I recall lying on the floor one evening watching TV with Linda when a Burger King commercial featured a double cheeseburger. Linda remarked that she wanted to get one someday. I quickly piped in to inform her that these things are on TV commercials. They were not real. Just pretend.

Another occasion that showed my lack of awareness about what others had happened during nutrition week at school in third grade. The teacher had the children to keep a journal of their meals for the week. At the end of the week, he went around the room and asked each child what they had for dinner the night before. One of the girls in my class told us that she had had steak and baked potato the night before. I knew that wasn't true because that kind of thing only happened on TV. Nonetheless when it was my turn to answer I just froze. I knew I wasn't going to say we had beans and cornbread the night before, so I was wracking my brain to decide what to say. I blurted out I had steak and baked potato. I was immediately mortified because I knew what both the teacher and the students were going to think and say. One child did pipe in and made a comment about my statement that made the class laugh. My teacher was kind enough to comment," If Tammy says she had steak and potatoes, she had steak and potatoes, and you need to mind your business and not hers."

I did not like my name. Occasionally, I would ask Mama why she named me Tammy, just letting the question linger in the air. "I mean, you named Linda, Linda Rose. It just rolls off your tongue. Linda Rose...it sounds like a bell ringing. But Tammy? Mama usually brushed off my playful taunts with a patient smile. But one day, after I'd pushed her just a little too far, she set down the dish she was drying and fixed me with a look that silenced my teasing mid-sentence.

"Tammy," she said, her tone soft but firm, "Do you know what your name means?" I shrugged, expecting some generic answer. "No." She pulled out her Bible, the one with the worn leather cover and dog-eared pages and sat me down at the kitchen table. "Your name," she said, flipping through the pages, "means palm tree. And do you know what the Bible says about palm trees?" I shook my head, intrigued now. Mama began to read aloud from the Book of Revelation, her voice steady and reverent: *"After this I looked, and there before me was a great multitude that no one could count, from every nation, tribe, people, and language, standing before the throne and before the Lamb. They were wearing white robes and were holding palm branches in their hands." (Revelation 7:9 - NIV)* She paused, letting the words sink in. "You see, Tammy, your name means Palm Branch. In the end, people from every nation will wave palm branches to honor Jesus. The palm tree is a symbol of victory, of peace, and of triumph. That's why I chose your name."

I stared at her. The way she explained it, my name no longer felt plain or ordinary. It felt powerful, filled with meaning and purpose. From that day forward, I never teased Mama about my name again. In fact, I came to treasure it. When I thought about those palm branches in the Bible, held high in celebration and reverence, I felt a quiet pride that Mama had seen something in me—a strength, maybe, or a purpose—that I had yet to see in myself. Now, years later, when I see a palm tree, I think of our little kitchen, the sunlight streaming through the window, and Mama's voice reminding me that names are never chosen by accident.

We hardly ever had socks, and my shoes usually had holes in them. So, I would go into the laundry and find a pair of daddy socks, and using the washing pan, I would wash them. I would scrub and twist and ring them out until I thought they were okay to wear to school and then I would hang them on the wall behind the stove to dry. The next morning ~~getting ready for school~~ when we took the socks off the wall, they would be stiff. I did not care. I was ~~just~~ glad to have a pair of socks to wear.

Linda and I were just five and six years old when Jerry invented another game. It was a twisted ritual he delighted in, and we dreaded. He would order Linda, and me to stand face to face, close enough to see each other's fear, and then he would order Linda to pull my hair. I can still see her trembling, small hands clenched at her sides, tears streaming down her cheeks as she reluctantly obeyed. She did not want to do it, but she would reach out anyway because she knew she had no choice. She would grab a handful of my hair. Jerry would hover over us, smirking, as he barked, "Harder, Linda. That is nothing. You can do better than that." Each time, her hands shook as she pulled, and each time, it was not enough for him. "Harder," he would demand.

Then he would turn his attention to me, his voice dripping with mock concern, "All you have to do is say it hurts, and I'll let her stop." He made it sound so simple, like I held all the power to end it, but I knew better. I knew he wanted me to break, to see me give in. And I refused. I would have let Linda yank every strand of hair from my head before giving him that satisfaction. My scalp burned, my eyes watered, but I never said a word. Not once. Linda, on the other hand, was a wreck. She would choke back sobs, mouthing, "I'm sorry," whenever Jerry was not looking. Her apologies hurt more than the pulling ever could because I knew how much she hated what she was being forced to do. When the "game" finally ended, her fingers were always left clutching a few strands of my hair, as if proof of her guilt. Jerry would smile at her then, like a proud teacher praising a student, and pat her on the head. "Good job," he would say, as if she had done something worth celebrating. And me? I never cried. Not once. I never begged. I never let him win. But that did not mean I was not broken inside. I hated what he did to us; what he made us do to each other.

I hated the helplessness, the way Linda looked at me with those tear-filled eyes, pleading for forgiveness she did not need to ask for. I hated him for the cruelty that seemed to bring him so much joy. But most of all, I hated the way it left a part of us behind. Two scared kids trapped in a game we never asked to play.

For my first three years of school, we attended Catholic schools. Each class walked across the parking lot to church once a week. I wore a pair of patent leather shoes to school which were very slick on the bottom. When it snowed, my shoes and the snow were a bad combination, and I would often fall onto the sidewalk. Sister Mary B walked beside me so that she was able to swiftly help me stand up. She did so by yanking me up by my hair. The other children who often laughed at me and called me horrible names seemed embarrassed and saddened by Sister's cruel treatment.

When I was in the second grade a nun by the name of Sister Mauritia took me under her wing and looked out for me in many ways. One day as the class was getting ready for the school bus to arrive, Sister Mauritia called me up to her desk and handed me a sealed letter. "Take this home to your mother dear." she said. She gave me no indication what the letter was about. But I knew. I was in trouble. The whole bus ride home, I tried to remember what I had done but nothing came to mind. This didn't stop my heart from racing and my stomach from clenching from the dread of what Mama was going to think. I arrived home and got off the school bus contemplating hiding the envelope, but I decided I would be found out quickly.

I went out to the garden where I knew Mama would be. "Mama, Sister told me to give this to you". Mama looked curiously at the letter and headed toward the house. She washed her hands and then sat at the kitchen table, pointing at the chair across from hers. I took a seat and watched her open the letter. I tried to wait until she finished before I asked, but my fear got the best of me and I couldn't take it any longer, "Am I in trouble, mama?" She didn't so much as look up at me but simply put the letter on the table, took off her glasses, covered her eyes and began to cry. I was really terrified now. I couldn't remember ever doing anything that bad.

After she recovered, mama put her glasses back on and read the letter to me. 'Dear Mrs. Higdon, I wanted to take the opportunity to let you know what a delightful child your Tammy is. I would like to ask you to let me know if there is ever anything that I can do for your child or any of your family. I do not wish to hurt you in any way, but I have noticed that she sometimes comes to school in torn and stained clothing, and I would like to ask if I may provide some things for her.' Thoughtfully, Sister Mauritia. The next day after school, Sister arrived at our house in a black Volkswagen station wagon. She brought with her several bags of clothing.

To my great surprise, Mama offered her a cup of coffee. She accepted and she and Mamma had a cup of coffee and talked for more than an hour together. It was the first time I had seen Mama sit and talk with anyone other than family. Sister Mauritia and Mama became close friends and Sister visited often.

Occasionally, when we went out to catch the bus, we would find the same black bags on the porch. All day at school, we thought about nothing but the content of those bags. Christmas morning, daddy opened the front door to gather some wood for the fire. He motioned for us to come outside. On the porch was more than a half dozen black bags filled with wrapped boxes with the names of every member of our family on the gift tags. Although we continued to get the bags on the porch the years following, we never again found them at Christmas time. But we did receive an extra gift from Santa.

MRS. P

Our second move happened when the Catholic school we attended was forced to close due to lack of funding. Initially, I was excited for the change and was pleasantly surprised to discover, on the first day, that my teacher was not a nun. Quite the opposite. Never looking up from her paper as she walked into the classroom, she greeted the class in three-inch spike heels, a pencil skirt, and bright red lipstick.

Continuing to look at her paper, she set her coffee cup down and asked the class to take out a piece of paper and put our names at the top. She pointed to the large white letters on the blackboard. SPELLING TEST. This was my chance. I was a good speller, and I hoped this would be my chance to prove myself and avoid the kids giving me the wrong kind of attention. I didn't care about making friends or standing out I just didn't want to be made fun of. Not again. Not here. If I could do well on this test, maybe no one would notice my secondhand shoes or the stains on my dress.

I printed my name at the top of the paper and waited. I spelled the words in my head before I put them on paper. I knew I had spelled every one correctly. I wondered what Mrs. P was going to think when she gave me 100%. She came into class the following morning and immediately asked one of the girls in my row to pass out the graded spelling tests. She made no comment about my grade and that was fine with me. No attention was such a welcome change, but it was short lived.

It wasn't long before I yearned to be back in my old school. Mrs. P's morning routine rarely varied. She came into class reading the newspaper and holding a cup of coffee. She sat her coffee cup on her desk, pulled out her chair, and addressed the class. Never looking up from her paper, she screeched, “Take out a piece of paper and put your name at the top.” This morning was different. Instead of sitting in her chair, she perched on the front of her desk so close that I could nearly reach out and touch her. As she always did before scolding a child, she wrapped on her desk with her pencil. “Class, it looks as though Miss Higdon forgot to take a bath again.” I didn't move. I didn't dare look at the expression on the other kids' faces. I didn't want to know what they thought of me. I wanted to disappear.

I did not dare tell Mama what Mrs. P had said. I had seen her response when teachers were unkind to her children. I often came to class without a pencil because with daddy away so much, Mama was not able to get out to purchase such things. Some of the girls would let me borrow one but this morning none of them had an extra one to loan me. I was first to arrive in the classroom. I instantly noticed the desk in the corner had three pencils, one ~~of them was~~ barely three inches long. I walked over and picked it up, tears rolling down my cheeks. Stealing was one of the biggest sins of all, according to Mama. But I was terrified of what Mrs. P. would do if I came to class again without a pencil.

As I began to write, I held the pencil in my hand mostly covered by my fist, in a sad effort to hide it. I did not understand that this only magnified its small size. Mrs. P. rapped on her desk with a pencil. "Class, I believe I have discovered the class thief." I was devastated, but I managed to hold back my tears until I was on the bus. The last thing I wanted to be called was a thief and I had been called some very ugly names. Mrs. P. ordered me to return it immediately. The owner of the pencil pleaded, "She doesn't have to give it back. She can keep it." Mrs. P. wouldn't have it. She ordered me to get up from my chair and march the full length of the classroom to return the pencil. The owner of the pencil looked at me as if she wanted to say she was sorry but probably feared the response it would elicit from Mrs. P.

As soon as I walked in the door at home, Mama asked why I had been crying. I detested telling her, but it spilled out of me in sobs. Mama quickly demanded, "Robert, take me to that school." I do not know what happened at school, but things got better for me quickly. Mrs. P even seemed to treat me kindly without effort. A few days after the incident, Mama asked how things were going in Mrs. P's classroom, and I told her it was a lot better. She responded, "I thought it might be." When I was older, Daddy told me that day in my classroom was the only time he ever heard my mama say the word "ass".

When he was barely a year old, Ann's infant son was hospitalized with meningitis. He was critically ill and at one point the family was concerned that he may not pull through. During this time, my parents went to visit him, leaving Vickie in charge of the younger children, including Linda and me. Jerry was also at home.

Trying to make the best of a difficult situation, Vickie prepared a nice meal for us, ending it with a strawberry dessert that our mama occasionally made. We were excited about this rare treat and eagerly ate our meal hoping to be the first to enjoy the dessert. As Vickie served the dessert, Linda asked for more before Vickie had even finished serving the first helping. Linda was determined to take full advantage of the situation. However, after finishing about half of the dessert on her plate, she began to slow down. When she set her spoon down and pushed her plate away, Vickie asked if she had finished, and Linda replied that she was full and could not eat any more.

At this point, Jerry began to encourage Linda to continue eating, and when she started to gag after a few more bites, he insisted she keep going. The gagging increased, and soon Linda was vomiting the food as quickly as she had eaten it. Despite this, Jerry continued to demand she eat it. He even instructed her to spoon up the vomit and eat it again. After a few minutes, Vickie could no longer bear to watch and stood up, pleading with Jerry to stop. Jerry stood up, grabbed a platter from the table, and broke it over Vickie's back. The impact caused significant injury, and Vickie suffered serious damage to her back. The impact caused a serious back injury that, even 60 years later, still brings her daily pain.

LIVING ON THE FARM

Although school improved for me after Mama's discussion with my teacher, she and Daddy ultimately made the decision to transfer us to public schools. They began searching for a house in town near the elementary school and soon found a farmhouse for rent in Clarkson. That's when we started attending Clarkson Elementary School.

The first thing Linda, Jeff, and I did when we moved to a new rental was head for the outbuilding and search for toys the previous tenants left behind. As usual we hit the jackpot. We found dolls for Linda and me, and Jeff found a fire truck he played with endlessly. Moving was like Christmas when we found gifts like that!!!

The larger school was a welcome change. We didn't stand out as much and felt more accepted by both our teachers and classmates. The house itself was like all the others we had lived in. It was too small for our large family, with no indoor plumbing and heated by a wood stove. But it sat on a sprawling piece of land that we were free to explore.

Less than half a mile from the small town of Clarkson, we could walk to the stores and, best of all, to the school playground. We lived there for several years, and some of my fondest memories were made in that house and the fields surrounding it.

We weren't alone on the farm. A few feet from our well was a barbed wire fence and beyond the fence was what we considered miles of open farmland to explore. It was about five acres. The field was home to an enormous mulberry tree and an Angus bull that, to us, seemed as big as our house. When he moved, the ground trembled beneath him. But what made him truly terrifying wasn't his size. It was his speed. I was sure that bull could outrun our car. The mere thought of him charging across the pasture, nostrils flaring and hooves pounding like thunder, was enough to keep us on the safe side of the fence, no matter how much we longed to visit what soon became our treasured mulberry tree. Daddy warned us repeatedly to stay far away from that bull. And most of the time, we listened.

It wasn't long before Linda and I settled into a routine. Every Saturday, we were up early and ready for a day in the wild. We headed straight for our mulberry tree. This was the place where it all went down. We met our imaginary boyfriends, Mark and Quenton there. We had long walks hand in hand, learned to kiss on the bark of the tree and even did some swinging (of the adult kind) because we both liked both boys.

This day was no different than any other Saturday, or so we thought. As we were crossing the fence, Daddy yelled from the back porch, "Girls, the bull is out today. Better stay on this side of the fence." Of course, we knew better. We always made sure the bull was penned up before we crossed that fence.

We waited until Daddy went back inside and off we went. As always, we carried one of mama's quilts, a quart jar of water, and biscuits left over from breakfast.

We would pick wild onions and make sandwiches with the biscuits. At the end of our walk still holding hands with our beaus and standing in the shade of our mulberry tree. Linda turned around to put the quilt on the ground so we could have our biscuit and onion sandwiches and make out with our guys. Linda suddenly froze.

She looked at me out of the corner of her eyes, careful not to move her head. "Tammy don't move. The bull is right behind you." She dropped the quilt and headed up the mulberry tree like a bat out of hell, leaving Mark, Quentin, and me to be eaten by the bull. I thought but did not say, "Be still, my ass!!!"

I darted toward the mulberry tree but there was only one limb that we could reach, and guess who was sitting on that limb. Linda!!! But, as usual, she had my back. She was as afraid for me as I was for myself. I learned that as she reached down with one hand and pulled me up into the tree right on top of her lap. It is not something I expect anyone to believe, but she absolutely did it.

After about five minutes, we began to yell for Daddy. Soon, we heard the old familiar sound of the screen door slamming. Daddy came out enjoying his morning coffee. "What happened girls, did you do something I told you not to do?" "Yes Daddy." Linda's voice quivered. "And I guess you want me to come get you out of that tree?" Linda responded "Yes.". Man, she was brave. He laughed softly, took a long slow sip from his cup and said, “Let me finish this cup of coffee and I’ll be right there.”

Another routine we came to treasure was our trips to the store. Now that we were able to walk to town, Mama would often send Linda and me to pick up a gallon of milk or a loaf of bread. Back then, we used what were called food stamps, a book filled with dollar bill-sized pieces of paper that you tore out to pay for food. Like cash, food stamps came in different denominations. They couldn’t be broken down into coins. If change was due, the grocer would write the amount on a small slip of paper known as a due bill. Food stamps were replaced in 1990 with the EBT card. Often, when Mama sent us to the store, she would give us a due bill or tell us we could keep whatever was left over to buy a snack for the walk home. That usually meant we were happily making our way back with a bag of potato chips and a Coke to share.

One day, as we were walking home from the grocery store, we passed the house of one of Linda’s mortal enemies. To our great horror, she stepped out the door just as we were going by. She taunted Linda over and over, daring her to come into the yard and fight. We were on the opposite side of the road when Linda suddenly came up with what she thought was a brilliant idea. “I can’t fight you,” she told Yolanda, “Because my mama is afraid, I’ll get run over if I cross the road.” I wanted to stick my head in that bag of chips and disappear. We took a few more steps toward home before I turned to Linda and said, “If you were trying to sound tough, that was a really bad thing to say.” But I guess Yolanda must have feared us, because she let us walk home, still holding our bag of chips and our half a Coke.

The stash of toys we discovered while exploring our new home wasn't the only surprise waiting for us. Tucked among the trees, the house was a paradise for pests. Mice, rats, ants, roaches, and flies thrived there. The mice were everywhere. Some mornings, we'd go to the water bucket for a drink, only to find a frozen mouse floating inside. One night, as I lay in bed with my arms stretched over my head against the headboard, something brushed against my hand. Then, to my shock, tiny sharp teeth sank into my finger. A mouse had bitten me!

Even sitting on the couch wasn't safe. We could feel them scurrying beneath us, their little bodies vibrating through the frame. I always kept a quilt draped over the couch, hoping it would be a barrier between me and the despised little critters. Daddy set traps, but they were no match for the endless waves of mice that swarmed the house each night.

The mice were bad, but the occasional rat darting across the floor was unbearable. Winter was the worst. The cold forced both the critters and us kids inside, trapping us together. At night, the kitchen was pitch black. To turn on the light, I had to stand on my tiptoes, bracing myself against the table to reach up and screw the bulb in. The trash sat just a couple of feet away, and before I could see anything, I could hear them! The rats!!, rustling and scurrying. The moment the light flicked on, they scattered, their tiny claws scratching against the floor as they ran in every direction, including over my bare feet. That was petrifying.

After a few nights of this, I figured out a plan. I would creep toward the kitchen, moving as silently as possible. Then, when I was two steps away from the light, I'd sprint, twist the bulb on, and dart out before the rats had a chance to scatter and scamper over my bare feet. Unbelievably, I learned to beat the rats. Eventually, Daddy put out poison, and that was the end of those pesky rats. It was also the beginning of a putrid stench of decaying flesh, but at least, that was temporary and much preferrable to rats scampering over little feet.

Roaches crawled over our dishes, cookware, towels, and clothes. Ants were just as bad. The most memorable and most disgusting thing about them was Mama's cornbread. She'd store leftover cornbread, uncovered, in the cabinet. Before serving it, she would break it apart, checking for ants. If she found any, she would pick them out before putting the bread on the table. And we ate it anyway and thought nothing about it.

With no screens on the windows or doors, flies filled the house. Most mornings, I woke up to them crawling on my face, stirring as the first light of day poured in. But to us, flies were just part of life. We didn't know any different because it was that way our entire lives.

Occasionally, Mama and Daddy would shut all the windows and doors, spray every room with Raid, and send us outside for half an hour. When we came back in, thousands of dead flies covered the floors. Mama would sweep them out, air out the house, and for a little while, we'd have relief. But it was temporary. It wouldn't be long before we were invaded again.

Mama kept the house clean. She swept and mopped constantly, wiping down every surface, but keeping things clean wasn't enough. The floors and cabinets were covered with ants and roaches. It took money to truly get rid of ants and roaches, and money was for necessities. It was only rarely that Mama and Daddy were able to buy products to rid the house of these unwanted guests and the results were short lived.

One cold winter day, Linda and I were out in the field where we spent most of our time. We had our usual quilt, quart of water, and biscuits. We were spreading out our quilt when Linda spotted a big black snake. Curled up in a perfect circle, we knew the snake had been dead for some time. A great idea came to my mind. "Let's take it to the house and put it in Mary's bed." We found a long sturdy stick and slipped it underneath the snake. When I tried to pick it up the weight was surprising, we had to take turns carrying the snake back to the house due to the heavy weight. As we neared the house, we knew we would get caught so we decided to wrap the snake in the quilt to safely get it into Mary's room. Sneaking in the back door, through the kitchen and bedroom, into the living room and finally into Mary's room, we were able to maintain straight faces, but it was very hard. Not laughing was pure torture as we thought of Mary discovering her little friend. We waited impatiently for two hours for Mary to enter the room. We squeezed one another's hands to help us stifle a laugh. Then it happened.

We heard the most delightful blood curdling scream and suddenly Mary shot out of her room and cleared the living room sofa in one jump. Mama, of course, horrified at Mary's behavior asked Mary what in the world was wrong with her. There is a live snake in my bed, Mama. I immediately piped up and said, "It's not alive." That was it, we were found out, busted! Mama turned and asked, "Did you girls have something to do with this?" We were mumbling all over ourselves, "Yes, Mama but it was dead. We carried it all the way home and it didn't move. We just wanted to scare her. We did not want her to die".

Mama walked into Mary's room as we followed closely behind. There in the middle of Mary's bed, the dead snake lay, head raised high in the air, tongue slithering in and out, slowly inching its way toward us. We were no longer laughing but profusely apologizing to poor Mary who said she would never sleep in that bed again. Mama went out onto the porch and retrieved our snake stick. Handing it to me, she held back her own laughter as she said, "Take it back to where you found it", and we did not hesitate to do just that. Our trip back was much quicker and that stick exchanged hands many more times than before.

When we were in middle school, Linda and I got a free lunch. That meant pulling out a green punch card when we went through the lunch line. It was a rare thing for me to eat lunch at school for fear of suffering the jeers or sometimes pity of my classmates. When I ate, I would find an empty table and sit alone during lunch, praying for it to be over. The smell of the day's meal wafting through the air was torture to a hungry belly. The lunchroom staff would not hesitate to call out your name for the whole room to hear if you accidentally went through the line with a full punch card which was often difficult to discern due to the careless way they punched them.

Years later, working as a teacher, I often saw children having their food tray taken out of their hands due to having a full card. The school system would not allow teachers to pay for a child's lunch at school, but they couldn't monitor a teacher pulling a child into her classroom to choose his or her lunch from the snack supply hidden in her filing cabinet. There is something wrong with a person who will take a tray of food away from a hungry child. Something unfixable-hopeless.

Since I rarely ate lunch, I was always hungry at dinner time, which was typically right after we got home from school. The dinner table at our house seemed to be the place where we aired one another's dirty laundry and the place where I was always in slapping distance of Mama. One night at suppertime, Linda and I were arguing at the table. With each turn, the ugliness escalated. I was determined to outdo her when the perfect solution came to me, one that would get a laugh out of everyone at the table. I had heard the kids at school say it many times and even in front of teachers and it always drew laughter from the other kids. “Eat me!” I almost yelled the words. Before anyone had time to laugh, I felt the sting of mama’s perfectly aimed slap across my cheek. It was years before I knew what those words meant.

Linda and I had the same third-grade teacher, Miss Skaggs, who was probably our favorite teacher ever. She had a son, Kevin, who had a massive crush on Linda. One day, as we were walking home from school, Linda told me that Kevin had said he wanted to “screw her bolts”. Naturally, I had no idea what that meant, but it sounded embarrassing enough to me, so I could not wait to tell everyone. Sitting at the dinner table that night, I announced, “Kevin Skaggs wants to screw Linda’s bolts!” Mama slapped me across the face for the second time. I was so confused. I naively thought it meant he wanted to fix something for her.

One Sunday Mama came to me and Linda and told us we needed to make a trip to town. She explained very gently that it was time for us to have a training bra. Everyone knew that was not the case. It was time for Linda to have a training bra. We were thirteen and fourteen at the time and it was ten more years before I needed a training bra. But Mama was kind enough to include me so that I didn’t have to suffer the humiliation of Linda getting a bra before I did. That night at dinner, June asked me what I was going to do with my bra. She told me I could put some left-over biscuits in it, and I would look like Linda. Out of sheer embarrassment, I impulsively responded, “Why would I want slut boobs like you and Linda”. Guess what Mama did.

June and I had our best conversations at the supper table where she lived to aggravate me. I guess in all honesty, we liked to aggravate each other but I was more cautious because she scared me to death. She would ask me to pass her the bread, and I would call her fatty. She would respond, “Rather be fat than skin and bones”. I would ask for the salt, and she would ask me if I hated my blood, insinuating I was drying my blood up by eating too much salt. She would call me a scaredy cat because I was a germaphobe, and she would pick up any stray animal and take it straight to bed and let it sleep with her. I don’t think there was ever a time when we didn’t have a clever comeback when one of us made a snide remark towards the other.

PLAYHOUSE

I got my love of wood and tools from my daddy. My first experience with the wonder of tools happened in daddy's shed where I found two pieces of two by four scraps. I grabbed daddy's hammer from its designated place and searched until I found a ten-penny nail. I put the two pieces of lumber down on the gravel floor and began pounding. Before long I had the nail all the way through the two by fours. I picked them up to find I had somehow turned two pieces into an even stronger one.

I was addicted from that moment on. I love the smell of daddy's shed. It was an intoxicating mixture of sawdust metal, oil, and dirt. The smell is still intoxicating to me. I decided at that moment that when I grew up, I would be a carpenter. My daughter caught the bug years later. I heard a consistent pounding in my bedroom. Crystal had found my hammer and a handful of trim nails. She had gone all along just above the baseboard and hammered a nail into the drywall.

My granddaughter, Layla, who was six at the time, visited me for the weekend. When I drove her home as she was getting out of the car, she turned to me and said, "Hey Maw, I made something for you. It is in the garage. It's for Mother's Day". I returned home to find a four-sided box nailed together with small scraps of wood in assorted sizes glued on each side. It sits in front of my fireplace still. Layla is now twenty years old and engaged to be married.

We had a big circular driveway with a shed at one end that had once served as a garage. I spent a lot of time in the shed just exploring, hoping to find something new. I was constantly digging in the dirt for something left behind by the previous renters. I was perpetually curious about the families that came before us. One day, at the back of the shed I was on my bare knees looking for rocks when I had an idea. The back of the building was soft wood and there was nothing I loved more than a hammer, a handful of nails, and a piece of wood that I could get a nail through. I ran into the house hollering for Linda. "I have a great idea, come on!" She quickly jumped up and followed me back to the shed. "We are going to make a whole house out here." I could always envision the possibilities. I could see objects and imagine how I could use them to make something better, something useful out of them.

I began to lay the plan out for her and before long, we were off to house-building. We pulled the weeds up with our bare hands to prepare the floor. We gathered blocks of firewood and sat four around for chairs and placed a fifth in the middle. I found an old piece of plywood in the shed and placed it on top of the fifth piece of wood and pounded a couple of nails in it. We grabbed two old hospital tubs and nailed one to the wall for a sink, placing a hole in the bottom of it for a drain. We placed the second tub on top of this one to serve as our full sink. When we were ready to drain the water, we simply poured the water from the top tub into the bottom one and let it drain into a plastic bucket underneath. Above it, we nailed a milk jug with the bottom cut off, upside down for the water faucet. We turned it off and on using the lid. We built a shelf by placing a piece of two by four flat onto the wall and then nailing a second piece horizontally across it. This held our dishes and cookware, which was whatever plastic or tin container we could salvage. We had a telephone made with the handle of a milk jug placed on the bottom that we cut off the same jug.

Our cookstove was made in the same style as our kitchen table. We placed a smaller piece of plywood on top of a chunk of wood, secured it with nails, then gathered four plastic lids of different sizes from old butter containers and placed them for burners with one nail in the center of each one to hold them in place. Our refrigerator was stacked with two milk crates. Unlike the one inside the house, our refrigerator was always full of food. Empty ketchup and mustard bottles, a milk jug, butter tubs, some plastic fruit we found in the shed. That stuff lasted forever.

Our 'house" was right beside the garden. It was early fall when we built the house, so we had watermelon every day for dinner, which we invented by taking the overgrown cucumbers and slicing them like a watermelon and eating the seeds and throwing away the rind. We spent hours and hours in this house, even inviting Mark and Quenton over for dinner on occasion. I miss our little house and if I had the opportunity and a little wooden shed, I would build another one today. Linda would come over and we would eat watermelon together. Mark and Quenton would not be invited. We have new boyfriends today and they are much better kissers.

TWO CHRISTMASES

At Christmas time, our tradition was to have all the children go to bed on Christmas Eve night, then Mama and Daddy would wake us up at midnight to open the gifts. As young children we generally knew what we would get for Christmas. Our gift was either a coloring book and colors or a book of paper dolls. Sometimes we would get a set of jacks to go with that. Most years mama would ask us what we wanted for Christmas. Regardless of what we asked for, we always got the same gift, a coloring book and colors or a book of paper dolls and sometimes a set of jacks. Mama always hung daddy's socks on the wall filled with an orange, an apple and three pieces of candy.

One Christmas when Mom asked me what I wanted, I was excited and very specific. I told her I wanted a baby doll with a soft cloth body. Those dolls were so cuddly and felt so real, and I longed to have one to play with and sleep beside at night. When I saw my gift, the box was much bigger than the usual size for a coloring book and colors, and my excitement soared. Maybe this time, I had gotten what I asked for! But when I opened it, I found a coloring book, colors, and a few pairs of rolled-up socks. That was why the package was bigger. The disappointment hit hard, and I can still feel it. When we got too old for coloring books and colors, we would get a little book of Lifesavers or a matching hairbrush and comb. There were a few times when we would get a little baby doll, or a cheap set of dishes for Christmas instead of the familiar coloring book and colors and paper dolls. No matter what we got, we were always so excited to get it! We didn't get toys any other time of year. Today the smell of oranges or apples will always take me back to Christmas.

One Christmas stands out in my heart. Every year as we passed around the Christmas gifts, I would watch Mama sitting and smiling as she watched all her children. I always felt so sad that I never had the chance to see surprise on Mama's face as someone handed her a package. I never saw her long slender fingers tear into the Christmas paper. Never saw her eyes widen with excitement at discovering the gift picked just for her. I wanted so badly to give Mama a present of her own, something I had chosen just for her. I started collecting cola bottles off the side of the road and turning them into the local grocery store. I saved my pennies for months, counting them multiple times a day and feeling excitement build as the holiday approached. When I had enough pennies saved up, I walked to town to the little pharmacy and carefully selected the prettiest toothbrush I could find. To me, it was the perfect gift. On Christmas morning, I handed it to Mama, my heart swelling with pride. Seeing her smile made me feel like the richest child in the world.

As the years passed and Mama's children grew older, the meaning of the holidays seemed to grow right along with us. Though she insisted repeatedly that we shouldn't waste our money on gifts for her and Daddy, we knew that we couldn't do enough. It wasn't about the price tags or the quantity of presents under our tree. It was about the joy of giving back to Mama and Daddy who had given us so much.

Despite her protests, each Christmas Mama would find herself surrounded by thoughtfully chosen packages from her children and handmade treasures from her grandchildren. And while she might shake her head and scold us for spending too much, there was no mistaking the way her smile grew a little wider and her eyes glowed from holding back tears. Giving to Mama and Daddy became the focus of Christmas, a quiet way of saying thank you for all the years of love and sacrifice. Daddy would have been content just watching Mama carefully unwrap gift after gift. But we could see the joy on his face too, as he opened his gifts. What great pleasure we had giving gifts to them.

As children, we were always determined to stay up all night after opening our gifts. The thrill of Christmas Eve and the magic of the moment seemed like it should be enough to keep our eyes wide open until morning. But often, despite our best efforts and all the excitement in the world, sleep would eventually win. We'd drift off one by one, surrounded by scraps of wrapping paper, new toys, and the soft glow of the tree lights.

The next morning, we would wake up, refreshed and curious, ready to dive deeper into the treasures we had unwrapped the night before. The scent of home-cooked food and fresh-cut pine would fill the house before we even opened our eyes. We were always awakened by the comforting sounds of Mama in the kitchen—pots clinking, spoons tapping against metal as she stirred and tasted, making sure every dish had just the right flavor.

Mama would spend days preparing for Christmas dinner. She made rich chocolate pies, golden butterscotch pies, and that unforgettable Jello salad—wobbly and bright, crowned with a layer of miniature marshmallows that melted just slightly on top. Daddy had his own specialties. He was in charge of the turkey and dressing, and he took immense pride in his fruit salad—a recipe he had learned during his time as a cook at Fort Knox. It was an unusual but beloved mix of fresh and canned fruit, fluffy marshmallows, and a touch of mayonnaise. It might sound strange to outsiders, but to us, it was a tradition. That fruit salad has been a part of our Christmas tradition for over fifty years now.

At precisely noon, Mama would call everyone into the kitchen for the feast she and Daddy had put their heart and soul into, and we would fill our plates, always coming back for seconds and sometimes thirds. The celebration didn't end Christmas day—we feasted on leftovers for days afterward, savoring the special dishes that came only once a year.

Another Christmas, when I was about ten, was not so merry. The air was thick with the smell of Mama's cooking. She had been at it all day, just like every Christmas. Our tradition was always the same: gifts on Christmas Eve, dinner Christmas Day. This year, Jerry's little boys were there and were very patiently waiting for Mama to call everyone into the kitchen. They were small, fragile things. They could not have been more than five or six years old. They did not get much to eat at home, so I knew those boys were hungry. They hovered near the kitchen all day, their eyes fixed on Mama as she cooked. I could see the hunger in their faces, their tiny hands restless as if they could already feel the warmth of a full plate.

Finally, it was time. We all gathered around the table; the food spread out like a feast from another world. Mama said grace, her voice soft but steady. Jerry's oldest son stood there holding his plate, his eyes wide with anticipation. But just as mama's words faded, Jerry—the boys' daddy—broke the silence. "Let's go home." he said, his voice cold and final. The room froze. No one moved, no one breathed. Even Mama, who rarely spoke out against him, tried to intervene. "Jerry, please," she said, her voice trembling, "Let the boys eat". Jerry did not answer. He just shot her a look of disdain and without warning, he grabbed his oldest son by the leg and yanked him up like he was nothing. The hungry little boy dangled in the air; his wide, tear-filled eyes locked on the food he would never touch. Jerry held him there, making sure the boy saw everything—the ham, the mashed potatoes, the green beans and all the yummy desserts—before slamming him back onto the ground. "Let's go." he said again, colder this time. His plate hit the floor, shattering the silence with a sharp, hollow sound. Jerry dragged both boys out the door. We ate our Christmas dinner in sorrow that year, the joy, once again, was stolen from us by Jerry.

Mama made breakfast every single morning before we headed off to school. No matter how tired she was, no matter what chaos had unfolded the night before, she always managed to have biscuits and gravy ready for us before we went to school. Her biscuits were nothing fancy—just flour, lard, and water—but you would never have guessed it. They were warm, flaky, and full of flavor. There was something comforting about that morning ritual, like the one pleasant constant we could count on. But not every morning stayed peaceful.

I remember one morning especially clearly. Jerry came stumbling in just as the sky was starting to lighten, drunk and already boiling with one of his rages. That kind of tension, the kind that comes in the wake of familiar footsteps, always hit before he even opened his mouth. You could feel it in your chest before you saw him.

Three things from that morning burned themselves into my memory: First, Jerry—once again—ripped the TV from its stand and hurled it out the kitchen door like it was nothing more than trash. The crash of it hitting the ground outside sounded final, like a gunshot cutting through the morning quiet. Second, Mama had to start breakfast all over again, because the glass from a window Jerry shattered had scattered across the biscuits. I still remember her silent determination as she swept the mess aside and set about making a new batch, like even this kind of madness couldn't break her rhythm. And third, we didn't go to school that day. The house was too shaken, like even the walls needed time to recover.

We never had lunch unless we were at school. That's just the way it was. So, to miss a day of school meant going without a meal. Dinner, or supper as we called it, thankfully was dependable. It was usually pinto beans and cornbread served not long after we arrived home from school. It wasn't much but it was warm, ~~feeling and~~ familiar and wholesome. That simple meal grounded us even when everything else felt unstable.

One evening we gathered around the table for dinner. Us kids ate standing up because there were only two chairs. One for mama and one for daddy. Even if there had been chairs for everyone, our tiny kitchen couldn't have fit them all in. As usual we had beans and cornbread. Mama had her own way of eating beans and cornbread. She didn't crumble the cornbread in the beans or pour the beans over the cornbread like the rest of us did. Instead, she pinched off a piece of bread, pressed it into her bean soup with her fingertips until it was soft then used it to push the beans up on her fork. It was deliberate and almost graceful in a way.

That night, we heard those familiar footsteps, and Jerry came into the kitchen with a friend that I didn't recognize. Jerry was drunk as he often was and already in one of his cruel, mocking moods and we all held our breaths wondering who his target would be this time. Right there in front of his friend who surprisingly seemed sober, Jerry began mocking Mama. He zeroed in on the way she held her fork about halfway down so she could better smash her beans. He sneered that she looked like an animal scooping up food with her hands and stuffing it into her mouth. He laughed loudly dragging it on for what felt like forever. No one said a word, but we all felt the sting of mama's humiliation, as she sat there silently absorbing the blows. Eventually Jerry left with his friend, but the damage lingered.

Sadly, Mama's degradation was not over. A few days later, again around dinner time, Jerry came back, drunk again and once more with the same young man. Mama saw them walk in and immediately picked up her fork at the top and began eating her beans without using her cornbread the way she liked. This only gave Jerry more fuel. He mocked her, accusing her of changing how she ate just to hide her animal ways from his friend. He claimed she must have been using her hands until she heard them coming in and quickly picked up her fork to appear more civilized. My heart ached for her as she said nothing and just kept eating in silence. while he continued the cruel show. When he finally went away, we were left with our plain meal and a thick heavy silence. The food hadn't changed but the shame and helplessness that filled the room made it hard to swallow.

As if this weren't enough, Jerry poked fun at Mama and her bathing habits. He would comment about how often she took a bath, brushed her teeth, or changed her clothes in front of whoever was sitting there and the more, the better. Mama would sit there looking at her fingernails and waiting for the rant to end. To do otherwise would undoubtably end in disaster.

Through the kitchen and just outside that screen door, just a few yards away was our well where we drew water. One day I had the clever idea of showing the younger kids a skill I had perfected over the last few weeks. I was able to put my body down into the well and hold myself up by the crooks of my elbows. It was quite a show, and I had everyone's attention. Unbeknownst to me at the time, I even had Mama's attention. Out of nowhere, I heard the screen door slam. I looked up to see Mama coming at me like a mad bull. I knew that it may be a few hours, maybe even dark, but I knew before the day was over, I would be dead. I had never seen mama so red faced and mad. That was the last lesson I gave on hanging from the well.

OUTHOUSE

Just a few yards from the back porch stood our outhouse. When we moved there, I was excited because the outhouse was newer than the ones at our past houses. Unlike the rickety, drafty structures I had grown used to, this one had sturdy walls, a proper door that latched, and even a little vent at the top to let in fresh air. To most people, I'm sure it was just another outhouse. To other children my age, it would have been a source of ridicule, as I was probably the one of very few children in my school that didn't have inside plumbing. Some had probably never even heard of an outhouse. But to me, it was an improvement, a step up. It gave me something to take care of, a space that could be made neat and orderly, a little corner of the world I could control. I took ~~great~~ pride in keeping the outhouse as clean as possible.

Every day, I would take the broom and sweep the wooden floor meticulously, ensuring there wasn't a speck of dust or dirt left behind. I would sweep the seat as well, making sure it was free of any debris, and even swept the ground in front of it, creating a neat and tidy path leading all the way up to the house. I wanted it to be an invitation. (At least as inviting as an outhouse could be). One of my biggest projects was organizing the newspaper we used as toilet paper. Instead of simply leaving the stack in a messy pile, I took the time to separate the sheets into sections, carefully tearing or cutting them into quarters, and then stacking them into neat little piles. My goal was to make it easy for everyone to grab a piece without creating a mess. In my mind, if I could make the outhouse tidy, then maybe it wouldn't feel so unpleasant to use.

However, my siblings did not share my enthusiasm for keeping things orderly. Time and time again, I would return to find my carefully arranged newspaper piles scattered, the floor dirtied with footprints, and my swept pathway ruined. It frustrated me to no end, but I refused to give up. I would sigh, grab the broom, and start again, determined to restore order. The outhouse presented different challenges depending on the season. In the summer, it could be unbearably hot, and the buzzing of flies made every visit a test of endurance. I did my best to combat the problem by leaving the door open when it wasn't in use, hoping to air it out. In the winter, the experience was even worse, the cold would seep into the wooden walls, and sitting on the seat was like perching on a block of ice. But no matter the season, I kept up my routine, tending to this essential structure with unwavering dedication.

Looking back, I think my persistence with the outhouse was more than just about cleanliness. In a chaotic household filled with siblings, it was one small thing I could control. It gave me a sense of purpose, a task that was mine alone. Even though my efforts were often undone, unnoticed, and unappreciated, I never let it deter me. Instead, I saw it as my way of bringing a little order to our lives, a small attempt to soften the harsh realitiy of the poverty we lived in. It gave me something to take care of, a space that could be made neat and orderly, a little corner of the world I could control.

VANISHING ACTS

One morning, I was standing in the kitchen watching mama get ready to make breakfast. She had a stove burner on high temperature to melt the lard for her biscuits. Mary and Jerry were sitting at the table. Mary was scrubbing the stains from the coffee pot and Jerry was drinking coffee and smoking a cigarette. I told mama I was cold, and she told me to go stand by the fire. Jerry piped in and said, "Come here. I know something that will warm you up." I did not move. He reached for my hand and took me over to the stove and held my little hand above the red-hot burner. It is one of the few times I showed any reaction to his abuse. I could feel the heat already burning my hand as he inched it closer and closer, and I was trying to pull back and escape the terrific pain that I knew was coming.

Mama went on about her business but when I began softly crying, Mary slammed down the coffee pot and yelled, "Jerry, leave her alone." She stood, her chair scooting across the floor, and started toward me, but he had already let go and shoved me towards Mary. She put her arms around me and watched as Jerry left the room. No sooner was he out of sight than mama reached up and slapped Mary across the face. "You need to learn to mind your own business. He was not going to hurt her." But he did hurt me. He added one more layer to the fear and trauma that I would carry with me for the rest of my life. One more possible method of torture that I had not thought of was pasted into my mind.

Jerry continued to live with us most of the time and let his family fend for themselves. His wife was the daughter of a Baptist minister. She was very passive and naive but very kind. One day I was coloring in the living room and Jerry called her to come into the room. He was holding a large mirror in his hand. He put it on the floor as he whispered something in her ear. She teared up, look over toward me and pleaded, “Jerry, don’t make me do that here.” He gave her a look that left no doubt about how serious he was. She went into the bedroom and shortly came back out. She made one last plea, “Can’t we just do it in the other room?” He took the mirror and struck her across the back with it, placed it back on the floor and pointed to it. She stood with one foot on each side of the mirror. I briefly looked up from my coloring. Apparently, when he made her go into the bedroom, he told her to take off her panties. He made her stand there for the longest time, revealing her most private self while I colored in my princess coloring book, just inches away.

Jerry and his wife were separated for some time when Jerry got wind of fact that Chris and his wife had been together. He was furious when he learned of this. He was not used to being on the short end of the stick. The anger boiled inside him, but he was not one to verbally confront someone and have a reasonable talk. It was an attack. Generally physical, and always from behind. Jerry lay in wait for Chris, positioning himself behind the bedroom door, ready to pounce when unsuspecting Chris came in. He had nothing else to do and nowhere to go, so he waited.

CHRIS, DADDY,AND JERRY

Shortly Chris came through the front door, with no inkling that danger was lurking inside for him in the back room. When Chris finally walked through the bedroom door, completely unaware of the ambush, Jerry attacked. He jumped Chris from behind, knocking him down and lodging him between two pieces of furniture where he could not move. Chris had no time to react before Jerry was on top of him. Jerry was filled with rage, and it was directed at Chris. In an instant, Jerry was on top of Chris, his voice filled with rage. "I'll fix your pretty face. No woman will want you again." The kicks came hard, and fast. Being restrained as he was by the furniture, Chris was not even able to shield his face or to fight back. After a horrendous beating Chris managed to free himself from the two pieces of furniture and get out the front door. He went to a friend's house and stayed until he felt it was safe to return to his own home.

JERRY, DADDY, AND CHRIS

Jerry just went on, life as usual, waiting for his next victim, the next time he didn't get his way, the next time he found someone smarter than himself, or the next time he was simply in the mood for sadistic entertainment.

One particularly rough day at home, Linda and I were able to slip out of the house by making our way to the back door. Once we made it to the road and to the point where we were not visible from the house, we both felt a weight lift and we were free. I felt like I had lost ten pounds just having enough space between the house and me so that I could run to safety if I was spotted. We walked to the nearby elementary school where we often went just to swing our cares away.

We were both swinging as high as the swing would go, letting the air just blow all the bad energy from the house into a space that we could easily walk away from. "Hey, Linda, let's be Swiss cheese!" I explained the genius concept: we would swing as high as we could, and the air would blow through the "holes" in the cheese (a.k.a. our lives), and it would wash away all our problems. Linda, being the good sport she was, went along with it, and suddenly we were both on a mission to turn into Swiss cheese. From then on, whenever we had a difficult day, we'd head straight to the swings to practice the "Swiss Cheese Effect." I still do it as an adult, though I am not sure if it works or if I just look ridiculous in the park. Either way, it is cheaper than therapy.

One bitterly cold winter morning, we were getting ready for school. Daddy got up early to fill the stove with wood and make sure we woke up to a warm fire. The house was always freezing in the morning, nonetheless. We habitually huddled around the cast-iron stove in the living room, soaking in its warmth. The orange glow of the embers was hypnotizing, leaving us aching to crawl back into bed. One morning as I stood as close as I could to the stove trying to escape the morning chill, Jerry, sitting in a chair, his legs crossed, and puffing on a cigarette glanced over at me and smirked. "You're awfully close to the stove Tammy." he warned. "If you're not careful, you might fall into it." Before I could fully process his words, he pressed the palm of his hand against my thigh. My left leg came into contact with the scorching surface, and a sharp, searing pain shot through me. As I jerked away, a patch of my skin stuck to the stove, leaving behind a raw, blistering burn. Tears welled in my eyes, but I bit them back, forcing myself to stay silent. I didn't go to school that day because Mama didn't want anyone to ask questions.

Looking back, I don't believe he truly meant to hurt me that time. I think his intention was more about instilling fear, about making a point that would linger in my mind long after the moment had passed. Maybe he wanted to remind me who was in control to ensure I understood the consequences of whatever wrongdoing he believed I had committed. But in his attempt to frighten me, to drive his message home, he miscalculated. He either misjudged his own strength or underestimated the searing heat of the stove, and in doing so, he transformed what may have been intended as a mere warning into something far more painful, and far more real, leaving me questioning whether his intent even mattered given the results and the damage created.

When it was time for bed, four of us girls slept in one room in one bed, a bittersweet blessing. Freelon slept on a couch in the same room. Jerry occupied the third bedroom, when he wasn't spending the night with his wife and kids. We made do. I always slept at the foot of the bed, Mary next to me, her arm wrapped around my waist, not to comfort me but to keep me from falling off the bed.

One night, in the oppressive stillness, I felt her lean in close. Her voice barely audible, she whispered in my ear, "Don't move." I froze. She did not have to tell me twice. By then, I already knew what kinds of things could happen in that room at night. But I could not stop myself from cracking my eyes open, just enough to see. And there he was. Jerry! He was kneeling beside the bed leering at me with a sick smile. He was so close to my face that I could smell the cigarettes and bourbon on his breath. It took every sliver of control that I had not to gag. He was pressed up against the mattress, a butcher knife in his hand pointed straight at my throat. I will never forget the cold weight of that moment. My heart pounded so loudly that I thought it would wake the others. But the terrifying sight of that knife!!!

That was it. Something in me snapped. I screamed and bolted over Mary and the others, and flew out of the room like the house was on fire. I was well practiced in that. I burst into Mama and Daddy's room, shaking so badly I could barely form a sentence. Daddy barked at me, "What the hell's going on?" And what did I say? Nothing. Because God forbid, I rat out Jerry. But Mary was not about to let it slide. She came in right behind me, spilling the truth. And that is when it happened. Mama fell apart. She got out of bed, shuffled to her chair, and broke down right in front of us. A full-blown panic attack. Her body shook, her breath came in gasps. And suddenly, her breakdown became the focus, her trauma overshadowing what had just happened to me in that godforsaken room, and the evil man who was responsible for both crises.

As for Jerry? I do not remember what happened to him after that. He always vanished like a damned ghost once he had gotten what he wanted, the house locked in terror, chaos rippling through every corner. None of us went back to bed that night. How could we? We sat there, shells of ourselves, waiting for daylight like prisoners marking time. When the sun finally rose, it felt like we had survived a war. Relief? Sure. But we knew better than to think we were safe. Morning did not fix anything. It just gave us a few hours to breathe before the next round.

HIDING PLACES

We always scattered like little mice looking for a place to hide when Jerry drove up revving his engine. That was a sure sign that trouble was imminent. I decided that the absolute best hiding place was the space beside the refrigerator where Mama threw the dirty laundry until washing day. Having a houseful of kids, the pile was huge most of the time and I burrowed down in the dirty clothes pile to hide. When I heard that car coming into the driveway at a high speed, knowing it meant we were all in for a bad night, I would dart towards that refrigerator, and I would burrow and burrow and burrow, until I was completely hidden in those clothes. I was still scared. I knew I could be found, but I knew I had found the safest place in the house. Sometimes I imagined what would happen if he got mad and turned the refrigerator over or if he started shooting into the laundry, but what was I going to do?

Behind the house was another favorite hiding place. It was a favorite at night when we wanted to avoid being alone in the dark. An old, dilapidated barn that had a huge hay loft that was still filled with hay. Because the barn was so close to collapsing, us children were not allowed to go near it. We were good kids and seldom went against Mama and Daddy, but this barn, it was just too much of a temptation. We always went through the back door which was not visible from the house. We spent hours burrowing out the hay, making “rooms”, letting the loose hay fall to the floor. It was our secret, and we were never discovered breaking the rule of staying away from the barn.

The barn served another purpose, not quite so pleasant. When the terror struck inside Linda, Jeff and I knew to get together hold hands and run toward that barn. We never took time to grab a blanket or anything to soften the hay against our skin. Comfort was not a priority. We had our rooms burrowed back so far, we believed we could not be found. We were safe! That was our priority.

Sometimes, instead of running to the barn, we joined our hands and ran the quarter mile to our closest neighbor. Robbie lived in a small mobile home, right on the edge of the road. It was just big enough for one person, always immaculately kept, with a swept porch and clean windows. Robbie was quiet, kept to himself, and never made a fuss about anything. He never pried into other people's business. But he knew if he heard a knock in the middle of the night, to always answer. No questions, he just opened the door and let us in. The three of us, barefoot, cold, and too young to be out alone in the middle of the night, would file inside and sit on his couch, legs dangling over the edge, red from the chill.

We never had shoes, never had jackets. There was no time for that. When we needed to get away, we just ran. His home was quiet, with the faint smell of coffee and aftershave. The couch was stiff and worn but familiar, and he never minded us sitting there. He usually didn't say much, just sat in his chair. We never talked to Robbie about why we were there, three children, barefoot, cold, and scared, praying he would answer the door. And he always did, sometimes offering us a bottled Coke, split three ways and poured into coffee cups. It was such a wonderful distraction from what we had escaped. We were safe and warm, but we couldn't help worrying about Mama and Daddy and the sisters we left behind. Even though we were the youngest, with shoulders too small to hold all that weight, we were well practiced in worrying and we were aware of the things the others might be enduring.

We stayed until daylight. He never told us to leave, just waited until the sun came up and then gave us a small nod toward the door. That was our cue. It was safe to go home. Robbie has been gone for fifty years now. His little trailer is long gone, too, but I still remember those nights, the way he quietly looked out for us without ever asking why. He was an angel then, and I have no doubt; he is an angel now.

On summer weekends, when daddy had a steady paycheck, Mama and daddy would go to town and get groceries for the week. Most weekends were special because we could look forward to a special dinner on Friday and Saturday. Bologna sandwiches on Friday and Mama's fried chicken on Saturday. I remember getting up on Sunday morning and rushing into the kitchen for a cold piece of fried chicken that mama would put in the fridge for me. It was the back; my favorite piece and I was the only one in the family that would eat it. Mama raised and killed her own chickens, and I would not touch that stuff, if I knew she killed it at home. When I came home from school and found mama frying chicken, I would ask her, “Is that killed chicken or real chicken?” Mama would just laugh and lie to me because she knew how much I loved real chicken. It was not that I cared that much about the chickens. I just could not get past the smell when mama placed it in the boiling water to remove the feathers.

A GOOD SIDE

Jerry was not always bad. One Christmas when daddy was making a fruit salad, Jerry and I were sitting and watching him. Jerry asked me if I liked it. I told him that I loved the fruit but didn't like the mayonnaise mixed with it. He stood up and gathered a bowl full of fruit salad and went and rinsed the mayonnaise off it and said, “Here, now you can have fruit salad”.

I recall one night, pacing the floor fiddling with a loose tooth, which was causing me a great deal of anxiety. Surprisingly, Jerry noticed and asked me if I was worried about my tooth. I was afraid to answer, but then he followed up asking me if I was afraid that I would go to bed and the tooth would come out and cause me to choke in my sleep. That was exactly what I was worried about! I answered him with a very timid “Yes”. He told me that he could pull it out and that I would never feel it. He said he could do it without even being in the room with me.

He took a piece of string and asked me if he could tie it around my tooth. I nodded my head, and he proceeded to very gently tie the string to my tooth. He said now I'm going to bed and in just a minute your tooth will be out without me ever touching the string. He told me it was magic. He took the other end of the string and tied it to the doorknob. Again, he promised he would not touch the string. He finished, saying that he was going to bed and by the time he was in bed, the tooth would be out. He said good night, went into his bedroom, and closed the door. Like magic, my tooth was on the floor. And I didn't even feel it! Thanks to Jerry, I could go to bed with no fear of going to sleep.

Across the road from our house was a small pond where the older ones sometimes went fishing. One day I decided to try my hand at fishing. I tied a string to a stick and began to continuously throw it into the water. I was patient, knowing that it was just a matter of time until I caught a fish. I threw the string over and over and over. I was quite the fisherman. Jerry came outside and standing on the porch drinking a cup of coffee, he spotted me across the road, trying to catch a fish. He laughed as he asked if I was having any luck.

Then, amazingly, he said, "Let me show you how to make a real fishing pole. He went into the house and soon came back with a spool of fishing string and a hook. He took out his pocketknife and cut a thick stalk from the reeds growing at the edge of the pond. He tied the string to the stalk, tied the hook on and even went so far as to find a handful of worms for me. I caught my first fish that day. I can still see the joy in his eyes when he saw it flapping back and forth at the end of my pole.

One morning I got up to find the area in front of our porch littered with cigarette butts and rubbish. I would always get the broom and sweep the yard when I found it like that. I carefully cleared the area and continued down our sidewalk and to the driveway. Mama sat on the edge of the porch having her morning cup of coffee.

Jerry appeared just as I was finishing up. "Did you do all this?" He asked. I nodded "yes". "Mama, look at what a beautiful job she did. This looks so much better." I did something that Jerry approved of. What a good morning!

Daddy was a construction worker by trade, specializing in concrete. He was a small man, standing no more than five feet, eight inches tall. He was muscular and his arms and hands were strong from years of lifting heavy blocks. One day at work, he bent to pick up a five-gallon bucket filled with mortar, something he had done countless times. This time, when he turned to head back to his project, his body turned but his foot remained planted. Daddy filled us in on the details of the injury when he returned home from the hospital. "A sickening snap echoed through the site. His knee was shattered. His coworkers heard Daddy when he yelled out in pain. They came running and seeing Daddy's condition, helped him to one of their cars and drove him to the hospital. He was rushed into surgery, where doctors worked to repair the damage". Daddy was never the same after the accident. He walked with a deep limp and was unable to return to construction work.

With no income, times were harder than ever. Desperate, Daddy sought legal help and by some stroke of fortune his attorney won a settlement and a considerable sum of money. It wasn't wealth, but it was enough to change our lives. The first thing my parents did was buy a house; a brick ranch just outside of town. This house was our first real home. It had three bedrooms and, most importantly, our very first indoor plumbing. No more trips to the outhouse in the cold. No more carrying water buckets back from the well. No more hauling arm loads of firewood.

SHOPPING SPREE

Mama, always careful with money, surprised Linda and me with an unimaginable gift. For the first time in our lives, we went shopping for brand-new clothes. Each of us was given two hundred dollars, an amount that felt like pure magic. I had never owned anything new. We wore only hand-me downs from neighbors, or the clothes donated to our school that some of the nuns would bag up and secretly drop off on our porch. The feeling of stepping into a store and choosing something new, just for me, was unfamiliar and intimidating.

I was in completely new territory as I ran my fingers over crisp new clothes, mesmerized by the bright colors and softness of the new fabric. I still remember the items I purchased, a pair of burgundy corduroy pants, a mauve and pink striped sweater, and a pair of green knee boots. I slipped my feet into those new boots, noting how they felt different when unsoiled and free of sweat. They smelled better too! I stood in front of the socks display forever, touching every pair to find the softest ones to wear with my new boots. Mama had chosen Holly Hobby sheets for our bed and let us purchase a Holly Hobby figurine to match. Mama never rushed us. She allowed us to wander through the aisles until we saw everything in the department store. I know that she was just as happy to see our pleasure and awe as we were to experience it.

My senses were overloaded with all the choices. For once, we weren't just making do. We had something of our own. These things weren't meant for someone like me and yet, here I was. Finally, Linda and I were ready to pay for our choices. Exhausted, yet exhilarated, we headed home to our new house.

Linda and I shared a bedroom and were allowed to furnish and set up any way we wanted. We had a twin bed. It never occurred to us that we should have a bigger bed as we were used to sleeping four in a full-size bed. I decided early on that I wanted a chance to sleep alone so Linda and I had a routine. We took turns sleeping in the bed and the other one would sleep on the floor. Whoever slept on the bed had to make it the next morning before school.

I was always a neat freak and Linda, well, wasn't. She made the bed the first few times she slept in it and then it became a battle to get her to make it and even then, it was not to my satisfaction. So, the routine changed. I slept in bed one night and on the floor the next night. Linda slept on the floor one night and on the floor the next night. I would not let her sleep in bed because I wanted it made before I went to school. I didn't take her turn, but neither did I let her take it.

Across from our house was a cemetery and next door was a church. Behind the church was the house of a local business owner who happened to also be the father of my best school friend since third grade, Vanda. We were in eighth grade when we moved next to her, I spent a lot of time at their house but did so while her parents were at work. Her father was a gentle and quiet man. Her mother? Not so much. She did not care for me and made sure I left the house as soon as she came home. She was not crazy about her daughter spending so much time with a Catholic girl. Worse than that, I wore shorts! Vanda had two brothers, and I was just at the age to start noticing boys. Vanda's mom may have caught on to that and was fearing for her innocent boys against a shorts-wearing floozy like me.

The best thing of all about living next door to Vanda was that her brothers were friends with Charlie, the love of my young life. He had no idea whatsoever that I even existed, but I had enough love for both of us, and I didn't mind as long as I could look at him. He seemed to notice Linda more than me. I even walked in on them kissing one day. It meant nothing and I knew it. We looked so much alike, he probably thought he was kissing me.

Vanda and I did everything together. That is until we started high school, and Vanda met some new friends. These were girls that were not going to hang out with me. In fact, they made fun of me right in front of her. It was not long before Vanda slowly started pulling away from me and hanging out and doing things with them. Eventually Vanda stopped speaking to me at all. She would pass me in the hall with her girlfriends and laugh at me right along with them. Vanda had been my best friend starting in third grade. I do not know what happened inside her to make her start treating me so cruelly in high school. I won't even speculate. But when my friendship with her ended, it was heartbreaking. It was one of the worst break ups of my life.

During this time, I had a pair of shoes that had a partially detached sole so when I walked, I would drag my foot so my sole would not make a flip flop noise. I faked a limp to make people believe that my foot was sore. Vanda met me in the hall at school with one of her new friends and after seeing me dragging my foot. She smiled and said, "You are not fooling anybody. Everybody knows that your shoe is falling apart". I stood there silently, embarrassed and ashamed, but mostly wondering what had happened to my best friend to make her treat me this way. I was so degraded by her mean comment that I could not think of a response. I went into the bathroom and tried to think of a way to keep my sole from separating from my shoe with every step. I decided to just pull it off. This left me with an uneven height to my shoes but at least they didn't make a noise, and this drew less attention.

During my sophomore year, I did not have a coat. This was another reason for my classmates to shame me. This was during the time when the fashion for girls was overalls and oversized men's shirts. I wore one of my daddy's shirts just like the other girls. It was not about style for me. I was never able to keep up with that. For me, it was about keeping warm. It was the closest thing I had to a coat, and we had a good distance to walk and then had to wait at the bus stop. I was often asked why I didn't wear a coat. Not out of concern but just to humiliate me and watch me struggle to come up with an answer. I generally just said that I didn't often get cold. It was the best I could do without telling the truth. Lying made me sick to my stomach.

One night I got in late, and Linda was already in bed. It was my turn to sleep there, but she was already fast asleep and I didn't have the heart to wake her, so I decided to let her be. I would just sleep on the floor. I grabbed a blanket from the closet and spread it on the floor and went back to grab a pillow. Just as I got to the pillow, standing near the head of our bed, Linda woke up. She looked at me, eyes wide with surprise, she screamed "You were going to kill me!!" I started laughing, trying to explain that I was getting ready to lie down on the floor. She would not have it. She ran out of the room to report my attempted murder to Mama and Daddy who told her to go back to bed. I believe that maybe even now, Linda thinks I was going to kill her for sleeping in the bed when it was my turn to do so.

We did not live in this house for long. The neighbors were very unkind to us and were not ready for a couple with seven kids. We were not the kind of family that lived in that neighborhood.

"Bicycle Built for Two"

Daddy found a house back in Clarkson, that Mama fell in love with. It had three bedrooms and even had a laundry room next to the bath. It had a huge wrap-around porch that daddy broke up to add another bedroom. That room eventually became Jerry's room. This is the house where Mama would spend the rest of her life. She never left the house for the last ten years of her life. She would go to the front door and pull back the curtain just enough to see what was visible. That is as close as she got to the outside world.

Daddy got up early one morning and went to his shop to work. He would not allow Linda and me inside the garage, which was unusual and especially difficult for me because watching daddy work in the shop was one of my favorite things to do. At the end of the day, he came in and asked Linda and I to come outside. Leaning on the porch was a bicycle. This was not just a bicycle. It had two sets of handlebars but only the front set was functional. Both front and back had pedals but only the back pedals would move the bike and more importantly, STOP the bike. We listened closely to his instruction on how to operate it. He said it is harder than it looks, but we were not worried. How hard could it BE?

We found out. It was not as easy as we thought it would be. We both had to fight the urge to do the other person's job. The person on the front was to steer and the person in the back had the job of pedaling and braking. That is not the way WE did it. The moment we climbed on, we both instinctively tried to control everything. Linda wanted to steer even when she was in the back, and I kept trying to pedal when I was in the front. It was chaos. The bike wobbled like a newborn calf, veering wildly as we fought each other for control.

The first ride ended in disaster. I was in the front, gripping the handlebars so tightly my knuckles turned white, while Linda pedaled furiously behind me. We picked up speed fast—too fast. I yelled at Linda to stop pedaling, but she either didn't hear me or was having too much fun to listen. When we saw the fence at the end of the yard approaching too quickly, I panicked and tried to put my feet down, forgetting that the brakes weren't mine to control. Linda, meanwhile, was laughing so hard she forgot to hit the brakes until it was too late. We crashed headfirst into the fence, flipping over in a tangle of arms, legs, and bike parts. Daddy came running out, shaking his head with a grin, and asked, "Y'all figure out who's in charge yet?"

It took us a few more tries (and a few more bruises), but eventually, we learned to trust each other. Linda stopped trying to steer from the back, and I stopped fighting her control over the brakes. When we finally rode that bicycle across the yard in a straight line, Daddy stood on the porch, arms crossed, nodding in approval. That strange, two-seated bicycle taught us more than just balance and teamwork. It taught us how to let go, trust, and most importantly, laugh through the crashes. And did we laugh.

In high school, I was extremely introverted. I had no interest in social events and even avoided one-to-one conversation at all costs. I was truly afraid of people and stayed to myself as much as possible. I had one friend. His name was Robby. We hung out after school and played pool. He taught me some self-defense and we messed around a little with boxing. He worked out a lot and was ~~very~~ strong and muscular. Right after high school, he left for the military. This was ~~very~~ difficult for me, and I grieved the loss of my friend for some time.

MY HIGH SCHOOL GRADUATION PICTURE

Some years later, I was spending the weekend in Clarkson and had stopped by to visit Mama and Daddy. I was sitting on the old familiar porch swing when a car drove by, slowed down and backed up. It was my old high school friend, Robby. Just before I left home, he had moved away to join the service but was evidently back. He waved me over and I ran to his car, surprised and thrilled to see him again. Since I had last heard from him, he married a girl in a class below ours and they had a couple kids. We chatted a bit about old times and how much we missed each other. He asked me to drive him to town to pick up a pizza he had called in. He said he just had a few beers and did not want to risk driving through town.

We took the back roads and when we came to a stop sign, he asked me to pull over behind the church across the street. He needed to "take a piss". I did so without hesitation. He finished his business and came around to the driver's side and told me to get in the passenger's seat. I laughed, thinking he was playing around. "You are not driving me," I started to finish, "After you have been drinking." But before I could get the words out, he picked me up and threw me into the passenger's seat. He got into the driver's side and locked the doors. I was so shocked by his behavior that I had a tough time processing what had just happened, and it still had not registered what was about to happen. He reached over and grabbed the back of my hair and pulled me to him and began kissing me. I was shocked saying "Robby, what the hell are you doing?" This did not faze him. It was like he didn't even hear what I was saying. He awkwardly unzipped his own pants and clumsily struggled with mine, but he couldn't get the zipper down. My mind was racing. I knew how strong he was and that there was no way I could fight him off.

A thought suddenly crossed my mind. and I pulled away from his disgusting kisses long enough to say "Robby, you know me better than that. I'm not going to do this in the front seat of a car". I poured a great deal of effort into a kiss meant to convince him that I truly had a motel room waiting back in Leitchfield. I told him to take me back to Mama and Daddy's so that I could get my car and then he could follow me to my room. The big army boxing stud-wanna-be, fell for it. We drove to Mama and Daddy's house. I got out of his car, made my way up the driveway, opened my car door, and looked up and flew him the bird. He drove away in a fury. It was several years later when I saw him in the local café. He sat there with a young lady. He looked up with a smile like he was truly glad to see me, forgetting that I would have been his rape victim had I not outsmarted him. I looked at his date and then back at him and again, I flew him the bird.

Just before I graduated high school, a group of family and some local friends started a volleyball team. It was my first experience with sports and surprisingly, I enjoyed it and was not too bad at it. We played every evening in the parking lot of the convenience store and after the game it was standard practice that everyone went to the deli and bought a sandwich. There were probably about fifteen of us, so the store probably profited from allowing us to use their parking lot. Everyone would go inside and order a sandwich. This would be around dinnertime, so everyone was starving by sandwich time. Everyone including me.

I, however, would never have admitted that I just did not have the money. I would watch everyone enjoy their sandwich and truly suffer from being hungry and watching everyone else stuff themselves. There were times when someone would not be able to finish their sandwich, throwing in the trash what their stomach couldn't hold. This forced me to hold back tears from so badly wanting what they just threw in the trash. I am often tormented by the insufferable feeling of being hungry and times like this contribute to my chronically worrying about my children and grandchildren having enough to eat. My greatest fear is rooted in the threat of hunger. My purpose in life is to feed the hungry and I am waiting patiently for that opportunity.

After high school, I became friends with Paula, a vivacious, bouncy brunette with a smile so brilliant you could see it from a mile away. She was the most full-of-life person I've ever known, always full of energy and always ready to go. We spent endless hours together, mostly just hanging out at one another's house, talking, listening to music, and forever laughing at nothing. Sometimes we'd go to the pool hall, but more often, we'd perch on the hood of a friend's car, letting the night air wrap around us as we lost ourselves in conversation.

Paula's mother didn't care much for me. She thought I was a bad influence. But that didn't stop us. After her curfew, I'd sneak over to Paula's house, slipping in through the back door to avoid her mother's disapproving glare. Her bedroom was tiny, barely big enough for her bed, which pressed up against the opening to the room. There was no door, only a curtain to provide a minimal amount of privacy. Our ritual was a simple one, that felt like our little secret. Every night, we'd raid her mother's pantry, grabbing a jar of home-canned tomatoes, boiling an entire box of macaroni, and mixing it all together. Then we'd climb into her bed, balancing our steaming bowls as we laughed and talked deep into the night.

Those nights were golden, simple moments made extraordinary by Paula's infectious laughter and the unbreakable bond we shared. She was the kind of friend whose energy rubbed off on you, making it difficult not to be happy when around her.

I had married and moved away and had been gone more than ten years when in 2003, Linda, with such kindness in her voice, broke the news to me. Paula had been on her way to pick up her kids from school. On the drive home, she lost control of the truck and crashed into a tree. She was thrown through the back window and landed in the bed of the truck. When help arrived, they found her son sitting beside her, gently playing with her hair, holding her hand.

I went to Paula's funeral to say goodbye to a lot of memories, secrets, and laughter that only Paula and I could have understood. As I looked at my friend for the last time, I saw my beautiful, bouncy Paula, the same girl who had once sat beside me, giggling and eating macaroni and tomatoes in the dim glow of her tiny bedroom. I wanted to do like we had done so many times before. I wanted to just walk out of there with her, away from the adult nonsense. So many times, we escaped from a room full of adults, holding our breath and stifling our laughter until we could get away and make our own nonsense. She was one of the best friends I ever had. I'll never forget her, and I'll never let her go away. She is alive and well and as bouncy as ever in my heart!

One day, I came up with an idea to make a little money. Linda and I decided to hustle the guys who came into the pool hall. We would start by shooting a casual game together, goofing off, laughing, and pretending we did not know what we were doing. Then, we would challenge a couple of guys to a game, offering to play for a quarter. Most of the time, they would raise the stakes to a dollar, and we would reluctantly agree. We almost never lost, but we were careful never to challenge any women, as we did not want to risk getting our butts kicked in a physical fight. It was all about the game, and our little hustle gave us a fun way to earn a bit of cash.

Daddy would occasionally let me drive his car. I would head straight for the school parking lot and listen to my favorite music. These artists were a big part of my life. Their music took me to a place far away from the fear and chaos at home. Johnny Cash, Waylon Jennings, Tom Petty, and Prince were my friends, and they never let me down.

I was introduced to Tom Petty by none other than my mama. I went to visit her one day and she had a radio on her kitchen counter. Just as I walked in a song started playing and mama laughed and said, "Tammy I have been wanting you to hear this song. It always reminds me of you." The song was Tom Petty "Free Falling". After hearing this song, I fell in love with Tom Petty's music. He was my very favorite artist and if I was listening to music, it was Tom Petty.

I was probably pathologically heartbroken the day he died. It was six months before I could listen to one of his songs. Jeff knew that I loved Tom Petty and from the first date until he died, Jeff would be playing his music every time I got into the car, but for six months after he died, he knew not to turn Tom Petty on. His concert was on my bucket list, and I got to see him once in 2013. I sat so close to him that I could have taken three steps and touched him, but I knew if I did, he would never leave me alone. He sounded just like he did back in daddy's old car when I was seventeen years old. Thank you, Tom Petty, for all those years of being there for me. If there's anybody that I want to see when I get to heaven, it's you. I had seen my mama and daddy plenty of times and I will get to them eventually.

One night we were all in bed when Jerry came in drunk and raging mad. He was yelling and raving, with daddy trying to get him to calm down and go to bed. He kept raving and threatening this and that. Four of us girls were in bed in a bedroom off the living room where all the uproar was taking place. There was also a door in our room that went out onto the porch. We were focused on the living room door so we would at least know if he came in. We were quiet as little mice and didn't dare to move a muscle, hoping he wouldn't remember that we were in the next room.

All of a sudden, the porch door slammed open, and he rushed to the bed, took hold of the quilt on the bottom hem and with one terrific jerk pulled the entire quilt off all of us while yelling some threat that I was too scared to remember. He just turned around and went back out leaving four terrified little girls exposed and trembling in a bed that provided no comfort or protection if he should decide to come back.

Often, when people hear my story, they question how our parents could allow such abuse toward their children. Another common response I often hear is,

"Why didn't someone take a baseball bat to him?" Things always look different to the observer, but honestly, I also struggle with those questions. I don't know why Mama and Daddy allowed this. I suspect they were afraid of him and afraid any attempt by them to protect us would only make things worse.

It is true that Mama and Daddy seldom intervened the way we wished they would. Maybe they felt helpless against Jerry's temper, or maybe they had grown accustomed to the chaos, resigned to the never-ending cycle of his return. Either way, the house became a place where fear lived alongside us, creeping into the spaces where laughter should have been. At times, daddy would try to intervene, but it always made Jerry's rage spike to a higher level. Mama would then get mad at daddy for his part in Jerry's hate filled escalation of violence. They were as helpless as we were.

As I look back with an adult mind, I realize they did their best. They abhorred seeing their children suffer, but the damage was always less when mama and daddy didn't fight back. Perhaps they chose the lesser of two evils. Be passive and let this thing play out and get it over with, or fight and prolong and intensify the torment. How can you fight a determined, rage-filled monster? Kill it? That would be the answer I believe most people would give. But Jerry was their son. Evict it? Monsters just come back. All they could do was tolerate it and hope for it to end with no casualties.

Life went on. We learned to adapt. We found small ways to reclaim bits of peace where we could, moments of respite in a world that often felt like it belonged to Jerry's rage. But even in those moments, we always knew that fear was never too far away, waiting for the next time he decided to remind us of his presence.

JERRY IN 1971

After Jerry returned from Vietnam, he continued to live with mom and daddy. Though he had traveled across the world and seen the horrors of combat, home remained the battleground where he was always a victor. In 1972 at the age of twenty-one, he married and moved out seemingly eager to build a life of his own, to step into independence. It wasn't long before he returned to Mama and Daddy's house, bringing his wife and children with him as if needing to show that leaving home didn't mean losing his position, and his claim to dominance over the household. His presence was a constant reminder of that unspoken need to prove his authority, even while he sought refuge in the place, he had supposedly outgrown.

This cycle of leaving, then returning, played out year after year. Jerry and his family would drift in and out of our lives, never finding the stability they needed; never truly leaving the shadow of our home behind. Jerry had four children, making them a family of six. During all his lengthy stays with mama and daddy, he never contributed one cent to help pay for utilities or cigarettes, or anything else. Mama and Daddy simply had to stretch their meager resources to cover six additional people. Despite the passing years, they remained trapped in a cycle that seemed impossible to break.

The fights between Jerry and his wife were loud, relentless, and unpredictable. Doors slammed, voices rose, and tempers flared. We, the children, learned quickly to recognize the signs of an impending storm. A sharp tone, a certain look in his eyes, the heavy footsteps pacing the floor. These were our warnings. When the shouting began, we knew to disappear, to find a corner of the house where we could make ourselves invisible so we wouldn't be caught in the crossfire of their fury.

One time when Jerry and his wife were fighting, Jerry took her to the outbuilding. It was late and it was very dark outside. We had no idea what was going on in the building, but every few minutes, she would let out a blood curdling scream. This went on for at least thirty minutes to an hour. When Jerry finished with his torment, they came into the house. Her eyes were red and swollen and she had a black eye for several days.

Daddy always called me hardheaded and rightly so. I was stubborn as they came and planned to stay that way. It was necessary to survive in our house. Sitting in the kitchen one day, Mama, Jerry, a couple of sisters and me, I got up and walked by Jerry. He reached up with the intention of pinching my barely budding breast as he often did with the older girls. This was one of his favorite sick games, but I was not in the mood to play games with him. I pushed his hand away, turned toward him and looked at him square in the face and said, "If you ever touch me again like that, I will kill you in your sleep."; a line I had heard from him numerous times. You could hear a pin drop because no one ever talked to him that way.

As I walked by him, I turned toward the refrigerator and looked right at Jerry and said, "Jerry, do you see that fly speck on the refrigerator? That is what you are to me and to this family. Something that needs to be wiped away, you are just enough to take up space and to be a little annoying and that's all you are." I don't know where it came from. It just came and I couldn't stop until I got it all out. His response was even more surprising. His face did not register anger, just surprise. I knew that I would pay dearly for my rambling, but he did not move or say a word. I often wonder if this was the first time it occurred to him that he was exactly what I told him he was that day. Nothing. Nobody.

Our brother took a particular pleasure in wielding fear like a weapon. He had a way of looming over us; his presence alone was enough to make us long to shrink to the size of an ant. Sometimes it was his words, whispered just low enough to make us doubt what we had heard. Other times, it was his actions: a sudden movement, a deliberate step forward that sent us scurrying away like frightened animals. He relished the power he had over us. He savored the way he could manipulate our emotions and turn our fear into his amusement.

One night in bed, after a bad "Jerry" episode, Linda and I were wracking our brains trying to determine what we could do about him. We talked about involving law-enforcement and we talked about doing things to permanently stop him. We decided at the end that we would contact law enforcement the next morning.

The next day, we sat around the kitchen table; Mama, Linda, Jerry, and I, having coffee in an uneasy silence. The tension in the air was thick, but we did our best to act normally. Jerry slowly dragged his coffee cup across the table, the sound grating against the wood. Then, without warning, he slammed it hard against the table, coffee splashing throughout the room. He looked directly at Linda and me, pointed his finger and with a grotesque, knowing grimace, he whispered menacingly, "Words whispered in the dark can get you hurt." My stomach tightened. He hadn't been in the house or even on the property when we spoke. A microphone could not have picked up our voices. We had considered that and spoke in a barely audible whisper for two people sitting side by side. There was no way he could have known. And yet, he did. A chill crawled up my spine, my blood running cold. Linda and I didn't dare look at one another. Somehow, Jerry had heard every word.

After several nights of waking to the sound of Jerry in my bedroom, I was determined not to risk it happening again. My bed had an old metal frame with thin vertical bars, which were painfully uncomfortable to lean against. I began sleeping upright, leaning against these bars to make sure I didn't fall into a deep sleep. After a few nights of this, I was drained, but the exhaustion didn't stop me from continuing the practice. Vonnie, Chris's wife was familiar with my bedtime routine and would often stop by my room in the mornings after dropping off her children at our house for Mama to babysit. It became a personal ritual of sorts—she'd linger for a while, striking up conversations about whatever happened to be on her mind that day. At the time, I thought she was just making casual small talk, but looking back, I realize her visits were more than that. She was checking in on me in her own quiet way, offering a kind of moral support I didn't even know I needed. Her presence was comforting, and her easy chatter helped break up the solitude I often felt. It was her way of saying, *I'm here,* without ever having to say the words."

One night, I was so tired from night after night of intentionally staying awake that I asked Mary if I could spend the night at her house so I could get a good night's sleep. She immediately drove over to get me. I slept on their couch, which was right next to hers and Wayne's room and asked them to keep their door open.

Lying on the couch, I faced the front door. Sometime in the night, I dozed off and was awakened by the sound of the front door opening. I opened my eyes to see Mama coming in the door. She was wearing a nightgown and slowly coming toward me, not walking, but slowly gliding toward me, her feet three or four inches from the floor. She stared at me right in the eyes the entire time. When she reached the sofa, she walked past me barely brushing against my shoulder and pausing for a few seconds, still staring into my eyes. She then walked behind me and stood at the arm of the sofa near my head.

I froze. I did not dare turn to look at her. I was sure that if I did, what I saw would be so terrifying that my heart would stop beating. I slowly got up from the couch and went into Mary's and Wayne's room and woke them up. I told them I'd had a terrible nightmare. Wayne told me to crawl in at the foot of the bed with them, so I crawled in between them and safely, dozed off to sleep. Years later when mama passed away, my sisters went out to purchase a night gown since that is what she wanted to be buried in. The gown they purchased was the very same as the gown she had worn in my dream.

My story would not be complete without a few words about a man who played a crucial role in my life as a child and all through my adult years. In small towns, it is often said that everyone knows everyone's business, and in our case, it was both a blessing and a curse. The chief of police was Austin Wooden, a tall, broad-shouldered, dark-haired, confident, and handsome man. He was not only the head of law enforcement but was also a ~~very~~ close family friend. Whenever I was in town, I would stop by the local café to see if his patrol car was parked there. If it was there, I would go inside to have a cup of coffee with him, and we would catch up with one another. If he wasn't there, I would go inside and wait. He would eventually see my car and join me for a chat. One day, as we sat together, I told him how much I appreciated everything he had done for our family and how deeply I loved him. He replied, "I love you too." I love all your family." This happened after my mother passed away. He told me he was sorry about my mama, adding "If I ever find out I have cancer, I am blowing my head off."

OFFICER AUSTIN WOODEN

Austin had come to my rescue on several occasions, not in an official manner but as a friend. When he learned of my well hanging stunt, he was furious. When I told him, I thought he would laugh, but instead he shivered and told me if I ever tried a stunt like that again he would take a switch to me.

When Mama was in her last days, she had stopped eating. There were two things she still asked for: snow cream and wild mushrooms. It was April, and snow cream was an unlikely request, but it was just the beginning of mushroom season and Austin was an avid mushroom hunter. He and I had hunted together several times. He came to our door one day holding a small brown paper bag. Inside were three morel mushrooms. I cooked them and took them to her. Holding my breath, I put them on a tray a placed the tray on her lap. Without hesitation, she picked up her fork and finished them off.

OFFICER AUSTIN WOODEN, MY DEAR FRIEND AND PROTECTOR

Seven years later, I was at work when I received a phone call from Linda. It was always Linda that called me with unwelcome news. She broke the devastating news to me that Austin had just passed away from cancer. The cancer had taken him so quickly that there hadn't been time to inform me. The news hit me hard. I didn't even get to tell my friend goodbye.

A few months after his death, I had a dream that I was at a party, weaving through the crowd, when I looked up to see him standing there right in front of me and staring right at me with that old familiar grin. "Austin?" I asked, confused. "What are you doing here? You are supposed to be dead." His face lit up, his smile growing wider, "I'm never going to leave you." he said, and for a moment, I felt as if he were still with me, that he would continue to look over me no matter the distance between us.

Johnny Cash

Just out of high school, I was working as a server in a small diner in Clarkson. I was in the middle of the Friday lunch rush and serving coffee to a table of gentleman that I had never seen before. The sound of the door opening caught my attention, and I looked up from the table just in time to see what may have been the best-looking man I had ever seen coming through the door. "He looks just like Johnny Cash." I was praying I didn't say it out loud. He came right over to the table I was serving, sat down, and asked for a cup of coffee. I retrieved a mug from the kitchen and poured his coffee, my hands shaking so that it was clearly obvious to the other men at the table.

Soon, "Johnny Cash" asked for a menu and quickly placed an order. I was serving his plate of roast beef and mashed potatoes when he made a very crude remark. He wondered what the mashed potatoes would taste like off my cleavage. The other men around the table looked as though they were embarrassed and horrified by his statement. I could feel the heat rising in my face as welts sprang up on my neck. In the end, he did not find out how the mashed potatoes tasted off my cleavage, he also did not find out how they tasted off the plate because I dumped the entire plate of food in his lap. As I turned to go back to the kitchen, I glanced over at my boss, prepared to gather my things and leave. Instead, I found her covering her mouth to hide her laughter. She motioned me over to her table and told me I looked like I had seen a ghost. She continued "Don't ever think you have to put up with that from anybody." As for Johnny Cash, it did not seem to faze him. He continued with the crude remarks, while trying every way but the right way to get me to go to dinner with him. He was hard to resist but his mouth was more than I could stomach. His name was Romey.

Romey continued to come in for lunch every day. He apparently got the hint and toned down his sexual rhetoric becoming ~~more and~~ more of a temptation until I finally accepted his invitation to go out for dinner. I was still dating my boyfriend of two years, and this was probably not the best way to break up with him, but I have to say I didn't feel a lot of remorse. He had recently spent much of our time together reminding me of all the things he wasn't going to do for me—buy me a car, buy me a house, buy me a refrigerator, buy me jewelry, marry me, wear a wedding band, have children with me, take me to a movie, or take me camping. He did all these things for his ex-wife, and she divorced him, so I had to pay the price. He eventually bought me an engagement ring. He had no intention of ever marrying me, but the ring served as a stop sign for any other man who got close enough to see it.

Romey and I started dating regularly, and in the Spring of the following year, I moved in with him, thinking I had found a way to escape the turmoil at home. But it didn't take long to realize I hadn't escaped anything. I had simply traded one source of torment for another.

Romey's home sat on a fenced acre just outside of town. Leaving Mama, Daddy, and my baby sister and brother behind was one of the hardest decisions I'd ever made. Even though my new home was less than a five-minute walk away, and I could check on them as often as I needed, the guilt ate me alive. I knew all too well that my brother waited for the quiet hours—when the house was still, and everyone was asleep—to play his sick games. And being so close did nothing to ease the fear that came with knowing what might be happening when I wasn't there.

In October of that same year, I learned that I was pregnant. When I told Romey, he appeared somewhat pleased. I however was devastated. I had already learned that this was no relationship to bring a child into.

ME AT THE AGE I LEFT HOME

MY THREE-YEAR NIGHTMARE

One late afternoon I went to check on Mama and Daddy and I didn't return until after dark. When I arrived back home, I was greeted at my door by one of Romey's ex- or apparently, current girlfriends. I immediately asked her to leave, and she just turned to him as if asking for permission. He nodded his head, and she grabbed her coat and headed toward the door. As she walked by me, I asked her if she knew he was having a baby, and she responded, "That means nothing to me." As I was closing the door behind her, Romey was attempting to convince me that she had just stopped by a minute earlier and was unaware of our situation. He had told her all about us and she was just getting ready to leave when I came to the door. Again, it didn't occur to me that he was not being truthful.

Standing in the kitchen after putting away the last of the dinner dishes, I looked forward to crawling into bed. I had made dinner for some of Romey's co-workers, and they hung out after the meal drinking and playing poker. Romey left the table and soon I heard him call my name from the bathroom. I opened the bathroom door and barely made it inside when he pushed me against the wall and put his hand against my throat. He closed the door and leaned against it to keep me inside. I was so stunned. It did not even occur to me to try and escape. He pulled out his pocketknife, opened it with one hand, and held it to my jugular vein and in a breathless, quivering voice said, 'If you ever screw me over, I will kill you. "This came completely out of left field. There was no warning, no red flag, just like that. I did not know what to say except that I would never do that. It would never occur to me to do that. It was not who I was.

The next morning, he apologized profusely, promising never to do it again. Being twenty-two years younger, much less experienced, and sadly naive, it didn't occur to me to doubt his sincerity. It really wasn't a big deal to me. I experienced that kind of thing or saw it happen to my sisters on a regular basis. What I had not experienced was an apology. This was a dangerous source of confusion for me. I took people at their word. I believed him without question.

It was the Fourth of July weekend and Romey drove to Indiana to pick up his two children to spend the weekend with us. There were preteens, a boy and a girl. They were good kids, and I did my best to have a good relationship with them and take care of them when they visited us. During this visit, Shana asked if she could have a friend over. Romey was going out, so it meant nothing to him. I also was okay with her friend coming. The plan was for her to spend the night. The friend's name was Tory, and her mother was a local florist named Sharon. Romey went to pick Tory up and then was out the door. He would generally tell me when he would be home, but I learned to dismiss it because if he left the house, he would not be back that night and sometimes not that week.

Nighttime came and he was not home, so I took the girls to the local diner for a burger. A friend and server there asked me if Tory was staying with me. I told her she was spending the night with Shana. The building where Sharon had her shop was visible from the large windows in the front of the diner. My friend broke it to me that Romey had picked Sharon up from there a couple of hours earlier. This came as a great shock to me as she had been dating another woman in town for years.

I knew Sharon well. I had been her babysitter off and on for a few years and was close friends with her son. Apparently, this tryst went on for some time. When I saw Sharon in town, she always spoke to me as if she was not having an affair with the father of my child. For a period, I went along with her strange behavior. When I had enough of it, she saw a whole different side of me.

Despite Romey's promise that it would never happen again, it wasn't long before the violence returned—more humiliating and terrifying than before. After a weekend with his children at our house, I was in the driver's seat as we drove them back to their home in Indiana. After saying goodbye to the kids, we were on the road heading back to Kentucky. Romey asked me to pull over and let him drive. He had a stop to make, and it would be easier to let him navigate the route than to have me attempt it. We headed to the home of his ex-brother-in-law,

His home was on a gravel road which meant a slow ride and time for me to take in the scenery. I was enjoying the view of the tree lined road when we passed home where a lady sat on a porch swing. I recognized her from a photo I had found in the medicine cabinet months earlier. I asked him if he knew the woman and he, surprisingly, told me it was Sadie, a former girlfriend. After he finished his business with his brother-in-law, we headed back toward the highway. As we passed the home where Sadie sat on the porch swing, something came over me and I nearly instinctively raised my hand and waved. Somehow, I felt like she would get, "*I know who you are, and I know you are the reason he leaves his wife and kids at home for as much as a week at a time,*" from my wave. She was the reason for all the trips back to Indiana.

He did not immediately react to my waving at her, but just drove on, until we got back to the highway. As soon as we turned off the gravel road and onto the highway, he started to pound me in the face with his right hand as he drove. He was forced to slow down when the car in front of us made a turn. I took this opportunity to open the door, jump out of the car, and take off down the highway. My eyes were watering so badly, I could barely see the road in front of me. He pulled up beside me, parked the car, and came around to the passenger side. Without warning, punched me in the gut, knocking the breath out of me, and sending me to my knees. When I went down, he grabbed me by the hair and dragged me back to the car. Several cars passed us and slowed down to see this shit show playing out, but no one stopped to help me. They just watched as they drove by. My hair was almost to my hips at the time, making it easy to get a nice comfortable grip. And he did. My shorts did little to protect my hips as I was dragged first over the gravel, then across the pavement. He threw me into the seat and was in the car and heading back down the highway before I could get my breath. As he drove the ninety-minute trip toward home, I picked the gravel from the skin left on my hips and threw it out the window.

Rodney Adam Houchens was born in Corydon, Indiana on July 27, 1984. It wasn't until later that I realized the quiet, haunting significance of that date. My first son was born on the 37th anniversary of Mama's first son's death. I wonder if she knew. I wonder if she relived that morning thirty-seven years earlier as she held Adam for the first time. It physically hurts me to think of the emotional gut punch it had to be for her. And that she had nowhere to go to cry or curse or scream the pain away.

Romey was at the hospital when Adam was born. I did not see him again until I was released from the hospital. His nephew drove him to pick me up because he was intoxicated. During my second night at the hospital, I got an anonymous call from a female informing me that Romey was staying with Joanna while I was in the hospital. The first year of Adam's life is mostly a blur. I was in survival mode, being essentially a single parent, responsible for two lives now. When Adam was seven months old, I learned that

I was, again, pregnant. My doctor suspected that my birth control failed due to my stress level.

When I was in my eighth month of pregnancy, Romey made a deal to purchase a plot of timber. He had to meet with the property owner, a man in his late eighties, to sign the contract. Adam and I were sitting in the car and Romey and the owner of the property were sitting on his porch. I heard him say something about thinking about it for a while. He apparently had reservations about dealing with Romey now that he had come to do important business smelling strongly of bourbon and obviously under the influence.

Romey began to berate the old man, and I knew this was heading in a ~~very~~ bad direction. I felt so incredibly bad for the man as he tried to get Romey to leave his property. I also knew who was going to pay the price for the whole ordeal. As quietly as possible, I opened the car door, got Adam from the back seat and with my eight-month-old belly, crouched at the side of the car and ran into the woods. When Romey reached his car and saw we were gone, he began to yell for me, warning me what was going to happen to me if I didn't come back immediately. I continued to put as much distance between his car and myself as possible. Once I was deep into the woods, I was able to catch my breath. I knew Romey would never get out of the car and come after me. If he couldn't run me down with his car, he would leave me. And he did.

Once again, I asked to use a phone at the house of a stranger and called my sister to come get me. Later that night, Romey went to Mama and Daddy's house to look for me and when Mama told him that they had no idea where I was, he held a revolver to Mama's head. I don't know how a person is supposed to respond to that kind of news. After this incident, I would never stay with family when escaping Romey's rage, I would drive around until I found a church or warehouse off the road and park there for two or three days to a week.

Adam was almost a year and a half old when we moved to an old farmhouse that Romey was somehow able to purchase. He made enough money in a year to pay for ten houses, but he liked to gamble and was ridiculously generous with some people when he was drinking. By the time of the move, I was about eight months pregnant, and it showed. I had a jeep that I generally drove with the top off and the doors removed. A friend told me one time that I looked adorable driving down the road with my dress pressing against my stomach and my obvious baby bump bouncing.

On one of his weekend trips, Romey was gone Friday through Monday. When he returned home, he was adequately inebriated. He had stopped in town and had run into my friend who remarked to him about my driving the open jeep and how cute she thought I looked.

I could tell Romey was upset when he came home, and I soon learned why when he told me he had heard about me running up and down the roads while he was gone and wanted to know what I was up to. I explained that I just took a drive to the fruit market. He wanted to see the fruit which was gone after four days. He suddenly grabbed a stick of wood about the size of a Christmas paper roll and drew back and bashed me right in front of my face. The impact loosened two teeth and knocked two completely out. It also fractured my nose leaving me with two black eyes. I was able to save three of my teeth but one was too damaged.

A few weeks after, we were having dinner with his business partner who noticed the missing tooth. He asked what happened to me to cause me to lose it. I told him I was carrying wood into the house and tripped and hit my mouth on the wood. He asked how a dentist fixes something like that. Romey piped in and said that we had an appointment in the next week to find out. The embarrassment of his partner noticing saved me from walking around with a tooth missing.

Crystal Lynette Houchens was born on December 16, 1985. Romey came to visit us one day and brought Adam along. I can still see Adam standing there in soiled clothes, dark circles under his eyes. I cried for Adam when they left. A nurse came to sit with me and held my hand, reassuring me I would be going home soon and that he would be ok when I got home. She turned on the TV to take my mind off home. Crystal, three days old, was on my lap as I sat up to watch the show. It was a Christmas comedy that I had never seen before though it was decades old. I began to laugh and progressed to laugh until I was crying. All of a sudden, Crystal started to cackle. Every time I laughed, she would laugh out loud. The nurse came running into my room and asked, “Is that the baby?” I responded, “Yes, she is laughing with her whole body. Before long, my room was filled with hospital staff coming to see the three-day-old baby laugh out loud.

When we returned home after Crystal's birth, Romey told me to get ready. We were going to visit his parents. I had a cesarean section with both my children, and I was getting ready for a one-and-a-half-hour trip and of course, I would be driving because he had too much alcohol in him to drive. We spent a night at his parent's house, then I drove the nearly two-hour trip to his daughter's house. When we arrived, she told me I looked tired. I told her that I hadn't had much rest. She took Crystal so that I could take a nap. Romey came into the room and told me to never embarrass him like that again and gave me a quick, hard punch in the stomach.

Romey left for another weekend to visit his girlfriend in Indiana. He never told me this was his plan, but I knew. I decided I would take this time to visit a friend and Ann agreed to let Adam and Crystal spend the night at her house. At around three o'clock in the morning, someone knocked on the door. I was sleeping on the couch, so I heard the knock, and a knot instantly formed in the pit of my stomach. It was Austin. By that time, I was up and at the door, I already knew something had happened to my kids. My heart raced, and I felt a cold shiver down my spine. I was barely able to stand as I begged, "Please, do not tell me tonight. Wait until morning." Austin reassured me the kids were fine, but he added that Romey had come back to town, realized I was not home, and started looking for me.

Someone told him the kids were at Ann's house, so he went over to get them. When she refused to hand them over, Romey put a gun to her head to force her. Austin added that Adam only had on a pair of boots, and Crystal was in nothing but a diaper.

I knew where they were, and I told him I was going after them when he responded in a way that left no doubt in my mind. "No, young lady," he said. "I'm going to get them." Without a cell phone to stay in touch, I waited, unceasingly praying that Austin would bring my kids back safely. Three hours later, Austin's patrol car pulled into my friend's driveway. I held my friend's hand and held my breath as he got out of his car. He reached for the back door, and I broke down knowing this meant the kids were in the backseat. He carried both children into the house, both dressed in diapers and one of Romey's shirts. Adam was wearing his cowboy boots that he slept in. This was in the middle of January, in freezing temperatures.

The next two years are not much more than a blur. My marriage continueed to fall apart, like a ship taking on water—slowly sinking, invisible to everyone but the one going down with it. Romey, always controlling, would never let me be on my own. I could go nowhere without him. At times, I thought I was suffocating under the weight of his constant presence. He made me feel like a prisoner, as if every minute spent apart from him was a minute spent in rebellion. I started to forget what it felt like to stand on my own, to walk freely with my head held high.

It was Adam's third birthday, and we were at his stepsister's house celebrating. He loved going there because Adam's favorite thing in the world was fishing and they had a big fishing lake. I was inside preparing food to put on the grill. Adam requested hotdogs and canned peaches for his birthday meal. I had just put his cake in the oven when it occurred to me to go check on him. Even though his dad and several other family members were outside with him. You can never be too cautious with a little boy, a fishing pole, and a lake. The lake was in front of the deck but was hidden by a small bank. We had placed lawn chairs on the bank so someone could always have eyes on Adam while he fished. As soon as I opened the door and looked toward the lake, I noticed there was no one sitting in the chairs. I frantically ask if anyone had checked on Adam. Everyone on the deck looked at each other and started running toward the lake.

As soon as we cleared the bank, I just went to my knees as I saw Adam floating face down in the middle of the lake. When I was able to stand instead of going into the water, I turned and ran back into the house. I took his cake out of the oven and started to open the hot dogs. I was in shock. In my head it was his third birthday, and he was there. I heard the door open and Adam's stepsister came in the door, holding him in her arms he brought him to me, and I backed up and said I do not want him, I am not going to take him. She said, "He is OK, Tammy". I went to my knees. She had performed CPR, and he was breathing. I went to my knees again.

He was still full of water. I ran into the bathroom with him, put him on the floor, locked the door and sat against the bathroom door. The family was beating on the door telling me to let them in and I refused, still thinking he was gone and that no one was going to take away my last few minutes with him.

His sister-in-law began to tell me he was OK. I asked her to promise and when she did, I opened the door. She went into the bathroom with Adam as he began throwing up water. He was getting back to normal, but we took him to the emergency room and had him checked out. The results were positive. He was OK. Driving back to the house, he reached for my hand, looked at me said "Mama, is there any more hotdogs left?

Years later, when Adam was seven, he was having lunch, a hot dog. This took me back to this third birthday, and I asked Adam if he remembered what happened. It was a day that began like any other. He was fishing and he dropped his pole. He was reaching for it, but it was just out of reach. As Adam talked, I could see everything in my head. Without thinking, he leapt into the water, unaware of how deep it truly was. The panic on his face would have been unmistakable as he struggled, his cries echoing through the air. "I kept hollering for you, Mama, but you didn't hear," he said, his voice shaking as he remembered the terror. I thought the story was over, but then he added something that made my heart stop. "Then three pretty girls in white dresses pulled me out of the water."

I couldn't process what he was saying at first. He spoke so matter-of-factly, but I could feel my knees buckle beneath me. The weight of his words, the memory of him almost drowning, hit me all at once. I fell to my knees, my mind spinning with questions. It was difficult to capture what he had just told me. So, I just accepted it. God had sent three angels to rescue my dear Adam from almost certain drowning.

Our next trip to Indiana after Adam's birthday started out well. Romey reserved a hotel room for the weekend so the kids could swim in the outside pool. We planned to go from there to his daughter's house and visit for another couple days and then head home. We arrived at the room and unpacked the car. The pool was directly in front of our room and the kids stood in the window jumping up and down with excitement as I unpacked their swim wear. We were ready for the pool and Romey still sat in the chair fully clothed. I asked if he was going out with us, and he said that he was going across the street for a minute to the hotel lounge and he would be back in an hour or so. My stomach tightened. My mind started spinning and mapping out our escape. An hour passed and then two and dinner time rolled around.

After a day in the pool, the kids were famished and asked repeatedly when daddy would be back to take them to dinner. I had packed snacks like always, like I was preparing for Armageddon. This was Friday evening. By Wednesday evening, the snacks were starting to dwindle and without a car and no cell phones, we were essentially abandoned. The hotel manager had made his second trip to ask us to leave. Knowing the situation we were in, he left a fifty-dollar bill with me on his second trip.

On the fifth day, a thought occurred to me. I had heard Romey speak of a "friend" who worked at a car lot nearby. I knew her first name and the name of the lot. My heart pounding, I picked up the phone. I asked the person at the other end of the line if I could speak to Lisa. To my unimaginable relief, she asked me to hold while she transferred me. Lisa answered the phone, and I bluntly told her who I was and the situation my kids and I were in. I asked her if she would consider driving me to where he was. Strangely she already knew exactly where he was before I told her.

We arrived at the hotel room. Adam and Crystal stayed in the car while I knocked on the door. Romey answered and in full view was the bed where his friend lay under the covers, waving at me. I asked him to take me home, adding that Daddy was in the hospital and I needed to get home as soon as possible. He briefly seemed to consider my request until the sheet flew off the completely naked body of his @#$%^. She walked over and put her arms around his waist and whispered something in his ear. He told me to go on back and he would be there soon to take us home.

Lisa kindly drove us to his daughter's house where we stayed three more nights. I was in the bathroom splashing water on my face before I had my morning coffee when he walked in. He pushed me against the wall and in in his familiar quivering voice and in a barely audible whisper said, “Don’t you ever leave me like that again.”

By this time, I had no feelings left and the one thing on my mind twenty-four hours a day was my escape. I had given up on the easy out of his dying and began to plan a more practical exit. After I left Romey, he played the prerecorded message in his mind to everyone he knew, “She took me for a million dollars.” It was actually sixty-three dollars that I had saved over a six-month span and buried in a hole in the field of persimmon trees behind our house. I also took a twenty-six-year-old sedan with a seven-thousand-dollar lien ~~on it.~~

It was not long before I noticed Adam increasingly blinking his eyes. This escalated to shrugging his shoulders, clearing his throat, and grimacing in a grotesque way. It was painful to see. It broke my heart. One day, he was playing on the floor and his facial grimace and shrugging his shoulder was worse than ever. I, without thinking, said “Adam, would you please stop that?” He responded softly ‘Mama, I can’t help it”. You could have pulled my heart out of my chest, and it would not have hurt any more. I told him we were going to figure it out.

That night in bed, I prayed and prayed. I begged and pleaded. ‘Lord, I know I am not supposed to make deals with you. This is not a deal; it is a promise, if you give Adam back to me, I will be the best mom I can possibly be to him. Please heal him of these tics and the trauma that causes them.” The very next day, on the way to school, looking in the rearview mirror at Adam, I noticed that his face was completely relaxed, and he was not clearing his throat. I whispered a quiet and sincere, thank you. By the end of the week, the tics were completely gone. And to God goes all the glory.

MY BABY BROTHER

There are plenty of people you can mess with in my life, and I'll stay out of it, but you don't mess with my little sister, and you sure as hell don't mess with my little brother.

Romey and I were driving through Leitchfield when I pointed out where my little brother lived. Romey had already had a few drinks and decided we should stop by. I knew it wasn't the best idea, but there was no talking him out of it. We knocked on the door, and it took Jeff forever to answer, which set the tone for what was about to happen.

Once inside, Jeff offered Romey a cup of coffee, and we sat down to talk. He mentioned making dinner, then went to the fridge and pulled out a round steak, proudly offering it to Romey. But Romey pulled some money out of his pocket, handed it to Jeff, and told him to go into town and buy four ribeye steaks to put on the grill. He pulled his keys out of his pocket and pitched them to Jeff. "You can take my truck," he said. I had a bad feeling. I knew it wasn't going to end well.

As time dragged on, Romey grew angrier, convinced Jeff was off making a drug deal instead of buying steaks. After more than two hours, Jeff finally returned, grinning from ear to ear, eager to show off what he'd bought. But Romey wasn't having it. Without hesitation, he pulled back and punched Jeff square in the face.

"Where the hell have you been with my ~~damn~~ truck? You out making a drug deal?" he shouted. Jeff, caught off guard, insisted he had just struggled to find the right steaks, but Romey didn't believe a word of it. He drew back to hit Jeff again, and that's when I stepped between them. Romey shoved me aside, sending me stumbling toward the kitchen table. My hand landed on a fork, and in a moment of panic, I grabbed it, turned around, and stabbed Romey in the side. Romey was so drunk he barely reacted, the fork still wobbling in his skin as he continued after Jeff. I finally screamed, "Jeff, just go outside!" He did, and I followed, my heart pounding as I made my way to the safety of a side road. I found the nearest store with a payphone and called Mary, asking her to come get me.

When I got to Mary's, I was frantic, pleading with her to find out where Jeff was, desperate to make sure he was safe. Hours later, he finally called to let us know he was okay. That night, Jeff came by briefly, but we didn't speak about what had happened. He was embarrassed, and I wasn't about to make it worse. For months afterward, I'd catch glimpses of Romey as he got out of the shower, spotting the three tiny scars on his side. And I won't lie. Every time I saw them, I felt a strange sense of satisfaction knowing exactly where they came from.

I continued to live my life under the thumb of Romey, never seeing a way out. Every now and then, there would be moments of freedom; like when I could make a quick trip to the grocery store, my only escape from suffocating control. It was strange, this freedom.

It was a blessing and a curse. It was bittersweet. For a few minutes, I could feel like myself again, unburdened by his watchful eyes. I'd walk through the aisles, looking at the familiar faces, and for a moment, I could make eye contact without fear, without the constant dread of judgment or the endless questioning that would follow. I could almost feel like the woman I used to be before Romey had wrapped me in chains. But it was fleeting, and reality would catch up with me fast.

A voice in my head would warn me, "You've been here too long. Go home!" That voice in my head had been with me for so long, it wasn't about a specific time or what I was doing at the moment. It was about a scar, about knowing that safety had an expiration, that lingering has a price tag. Each day felt like another round in a race I couldn't win. The fear, the exhaustion, and the endless cycle of explanations had worn me down, piece by piece. It was hard to remember what it was like to have peace, to have a moment where I didn't have to defend my existence. But somewhere deep inside, there was still a flicker of hope that maybe, one day, I would find my way out of this prison and find my true self again. I was a prisoner, and if I found a way of escape, I better take it!

When I returned home, the grilling would begin. "Who did you talk to? Who did you see? Why were you gone so long?" I'd stand there, exhausted, struggling to catch my breath as I tried to explain my every move. There were no right answers, no way to satisfy him, just endless hours spent defending myself.

Even worse, the interrogation didn't stop at bedtime. After drinking binge, he would sleep all day, leaving him restless at night. And when he didn't sleep, I didn't sleep. Caring for two young children and an attention-seeking Romey drained me completely by the end of the day, yet rest was never an option.

He would lie beside me in bed, watching TV, and watching me. The moment he saw my eyes close he would start. Poking, shaking, yelling, anything to keep me awake. This cycle continued into the early morning until he finally drifted off, leaving me with only a couple of hours to rest before the kids came into the bedroom, ready for breakfast.

A NEW DAWN

One day, Jason, Romey's business partner, cautiously pulled me aside, his expression tense. He told me he was scared for me. "I'm afraid if you don't get out of here, Romey is going to kill you," he said. I had already begun to fear this myself, but hearing someone else acknowledge the threat made it feel even more real. Then Jason asked, "Did you know Romey bought a high-powered rifle? He keeps it in his car." And then he added, "He was laughing at lunch about taking your car keys, leaving you stranded with a two and three-year-old, twenty miles from town, with no way to escape."

But Jason hadn't just come to warn me. He had quietly taken Romey's car keys, slipped away to a hardware store, and had a spare made for me. When he handed it over, his voice was firm. "Keep this hidden. Never let him know you have it. I always kept a bag of essentials hidden in the house. It contained outfits for the kids and me, diapers, a blanket, snacks and water, a few toys, and any cash I could squirrel away. I put the keys in this bag. I hid it away, knowing that I needed to be ready to leave in a minute if I got a chance to escape. I also knew that I better make it, because it was unlikely that I would get a second chance.

A few weeks later, I was outside sweeping the front porch. Our house faced a large field, and across the field, I could see Jason's house. Suddenly, Romey yelled from behind me, "What are you doing? Waiting for him to see you?" I knew then that it was going to be a bad night. The way he said it sent chills down my spine. His yelling upset Crystal, who was only two. She started crying, reaching for me, and I moved toward her. Romey snapped, "Sit her on the couch and leave her alone!" It was around 6:30 p.m., and Romey was on his way to passing out. He lay down on the floor and had Adam lie down beside him. He threw his arm over Adams waist and in his hand, in front of Adam, he held his new rifle. Crystal continued crying on the couch as I helplessly watched, aching to pick her up and comfort her.

CRYSTAL JUST AS SHE SAT THE DAY WE LEFT

For nearly an hour, Crystal's sobs filled the room as I waited for Romey to fall asleep. When he finally did, I called his name a few times. When I got no response, I crept over to the bedroom and opened the door. I went into the room and slid open the window, literally praying the entire time that he would not wake up. I got the essentials bag out and threw it out the window so it would be ready. My heart was racing, and my hands were shaking so hard that it made it difficult to slide Adam from between Romey and the rifle. I was in tears from the relief of having him in my arms. As if she was aware of the danger, Crystal had stopped crying, but reached for me as far as her little arms would stretch. I reached down to pick her up and balance her on my other hip. Holding my breath, I tiptoed toward the open bedroom door, all the while hoping and praying that Romey wouldn't wake up.

When I got through the door into the bedroom, I slowly and carefully closed the door with my foot. It seemed like it took an eternity to reach the window. I bowed down trying to avoid hitting one of the kid's heads. They did not make a sound as we cleared the window. My feet were on the porch. I was one step closer to safety, to freedom. I did not dare close the window, fearing any noise might wake Romey. I climbed out with the kids and ran across the porch, across the yard, and down the gravel driveway. Every step felt like a lifetime. I remember praying silently, hoping that if he did wake up and grab that rifle, he would shoot me and not the kids. My body was shaking, but I did not stop. I could not stop. I made it to the car with the keys in my hand. I knew starting the car was a risk but of course there was no choice. I started the engine and was out of the one-mile driveway and on my way to hope and freedom and life. Life for my children and me was beginning.

For about two weeks, Romey did his usual crying and promising and begging me to come back. I was not fazed by his attempts to sway me. I was, however, affected by the pleas to see his children, only because Adam begged me to let him see his dad. Crystal was mamma's girl. She was not concerned about seeing him. I finally caved and allowed his nephew to get the kids to stay the weekend with their dad. As soon as they arrived at his mother's home where he was staying, He called me to let me know I would never see them again.

For the first time in my life, I allowed myself to show my emotions in front of Mama. I never wanted to give her any more to worry about. I needed my mama to tell me everything was going to be ok. I went to her house, walked over to where she sat at the kitchen table, and got down on my knees. I put my head in her lap and started crying, "Mama, he has my kids, and he says I will never see them again." Mama said "Tammy, it's going to be ok." I believed her because Mama never said something she didn't believe to be true. I thought for some time about a plan of action. I decided the best course was to beat him in his own game.

When he called again, threatening me with keeping the kids from me, I told him I thought it was for the best. As painful as it was, I did not have the resources to take care of them. I asked him to please take good care of them. Three days later his nephew brought them home to me.

Soon after the incident where I lost teeth and had a broken nose, Romey was speaking with my dad and defending his behavior. One of my sisters later told me that Daddy responded that he knew how hardheaded I was, as if justifying my lost teeth, broken nose, and black eyes. I spoke to Daddy, and he admitted that he said it but that it was taken the wrong way. This drove a wedge between daddy and me that lasted the rest of his life. I didn't speak to him for many years, and he died without my saying goodbye to him.

I was devastated when Daddy took Romey's side over mine. My face was black and blue all over, I had two black eyes, a broken nose, and a missing tooth. How could my daddy look at me and tell that evil man that he knew how hardheaded I was. I am sure there was more to the story; that maybe my sister did not hear the whole conversation. Once again, I felt devastated, expendable, and not worth defending.

One evening, I was in Elizabethtown at Lowe's when I saw Daddy's truck pulled off to the side of the road. Some wall paneling had flown out of the back of his truck and was scattered in the road. I stood there and watched as this old man, my daddy, fought traffic, struggling to haul the heavy pieces back into his truck. And I did nothing. I didn't go to him, didn't offer my help. I was too wrapped up in my own emotions, still harboring anger over his perceived collusion with Romey. Maybe I told myself he would be fine. But deep down, I know that in that moment I failed him and the weight of that has never left me.

Even worse is something I have never admitted to my sisters because the shame was too much to bear. One day, when I was living with Jason, I was cleaning in the living room when I looked up and saw Daddy stepping out of his truck. He walked up to the door and knocked, and I didn't answer. I stood there, frozen, watching from the shadows, letting my own pride and unresolved anger keep me from opening that door. I watched him wait for a moment, to see him turn back to his truck. I hid and watched him drive away.

These are horrendous acts that I have lived with for thirty years. I can see him in both situations as clearly as if it happened today. I see him walk back to his truck. I see him drive away and just let him go. I lost countless, precious years with him that I can never get back. I have carried these memories like stones in my chest since his death in 2003. This is my penance for treating my daddy that way. For allowing anger, resentment, and pride to steal time from me that I can never get back. If I could go back, if I could undo even one of those moments, I would. But all I can do is receive the forgiveness my Father offers me and believe that Daddy forgives me too.

DON'T LOOK AT THE LAKE!

When Romey and I first separated, I stayed for a while in the house we had bought together from our neighbor. There were many times when we had nothing to eat. The kids would ask for food, and I had to tell them we didn't have any. One day, I found some cornmeal and sugar, so I made pancakes with homemade syrup.

Eventually, panic set in, and though it was difficult, I called my sister Mary and told her we had no food. Within an hour, she arrived at my house, filling our refrigerator, cupboards, and freezer. Soon after, I rented a low income apart in Leitchfield, which is just down the road from where my family lived. I furnished the place the best that I could. I was able to let Adam decorate his room to some degree. He picked out a comforter for his bed and when we got home, we learned that it was a size too large. I was in the living room unpacking boxes when Adam yelled at me from his bedroom. Mama, look at what I did. I fixed my bed. He stood so proudly as he pointed out that he had simply taken the scissors and cut the comforter all around the bed. He was so proud!!! The comforter was perfect indeed!

I made a trip back to the house to get whatever I could of our things. As I was loading the truck, I saw lights coming in the driveway. My heart started pounding and I frantically started thinking of an escape route. I knew it was Romey. That he had been lying in wait for me to show up at the house. As the vehicle came closer, I was relieved to see it was the neighbor's truck. He had come to see if I needed any help. We worked a while and then took a break leaning against a tree in the yard and having a beer. He asked how things were going and offered to help in any way he could, as he took a roll of bills from his pocket and handed them to me. I was not a big drinker, so the beer kicked in quickly.

Inhibition lowered, I asked him why he never married again, and his response came as a total surprise. "Because I know exactly what I want in a wife, and you were already taken." I could not formulate a response. He said when things settle down for you, if you want to, I would like to take you out for dinner. All I could get out was "Ok." He asked for my phone number, and by the time I arrived back at my apartment that night, he had already called.

Jason and I talked every night, and I dated him for a short while before he asked for the kids and me to move into a house he owned near where he lived. This was an old farmhouse, surrounded by trees and much more inviting than a sterile two-bedroom apartment. We were thrilled to be back in the country.

I tried a few times to get a job, but without any experience, no one would hire me. I was stuck in a cycle of frustration and disappointment, so I realized my only option was to go to school and get the education I needed. I started attending Elizabethtown

Community College, where I pursued an associate's degree in office administration. I worked hard to get that far but as I was nearing graduation, I realized this was not the kind of work for me. I was not at all excited about the future. One day, a friend mentioned enrolling in a speech pathology program at a college an hour and a half away. She expressed her concern about the distance and said that she would do it if she had someone to ride with. Without missing a beat, and knowing about speech pathology, I volunteered to carpool with her. To my surprise, I ended up loving the program.

We completed two years at that school and earned our bachelor's degree, then transferred to the University of Louisville School of Medicine to pursue our master's degree in Speech Pathology. After earning my master's, I completed a second program and earned a Rank 1 degree in Special Education from UofL's School of Education, which opened even more opportunities for me. It is good that I had no idea how difficult it would be to get my master's degree. Had I known, I would never have agreed to begin the program when my friend suggested it.

After about a year, we moved in with Jason who had a four-bedroom house nestled by a beautiful lake. For Adam, it was paradise. He would rather fish than eat, and many days proved just that. I had to take him a bologna sandwich when he refused to step away from the water. His hands still smelling of bait and fish, he would grab the sandwich without a second thought, his fingers sticky and slimy with the residue of the day's catch. Life there was good and simple, yet full of joy. The kids had endless space to run, play, and explore. They rode four-wheelers, fished, and swam in the lake. It was a childhood drenched in adventure and sunshine. I often watched from the porch, soaking in the laughter and chaos that came with those golden days. It wasn't just a house by the lake; it was a sanctuary where their imaginations could run wild.

It wasn't all smooth sailing on the farm. When Romey found out we had moved in with Jason, his former business partner, things took a turn for the worse. The kids would visit their dad and return with messages from him. One time, Crystal told me that Dad wanted her to say, "Paychecks are a bad word." It took me a while to figure it out, but I eventually realized it Crystal's way of saying paybacks are hell while avoiding using a curse word. I knew then just how much Romey was using our kids against me.

Adam was ~~very~~ close to Jason but each time he returned from Romey's, house, he would not speak to him for days or he would show defiance toward him at every opportunity. This went on for more than a year when it culminated in Adam coming home one day, getting out of the car, and running into his room and sliding under his bed. I went into his room and sat down on the floor and asked him what in the world was going on. He was silent. He suddenly came out from under his bed and ran to the bathroom, with a butcher knife in his hand, and locked the door.

Luckily, I had a key to the bathroom. I opened the door and again sat on the floor, his back against the door. I reached out my hand and asked for the knife. He immediately handed it to me. I again asked what was going on and he got down on his knees and said, "I know what you all are going to do. Dad told me that you and Jason are going to kill me because I know too much about you."

Jason had a friend and farmhand who went out in the middle of one of his fields and shot himself. Romey told Adam that we killed him. Romey also told Adam that they believed Adam knew about it and that he was next. I asked him about the butcher knife. He told me he slept with it under his pillow to protect himself from us. Adam was seven years old.

I pulled him into my lap and fought for fifteen to twenty minutes to get him to relax in my arms. When he finally relaxed, he began to cry. I asked him, "Adam, do you really believe I would hurt you? "No." he said. "Do you believe Jason would hurt you? "No mama." We would never ever hurt you. We love you too much to ever hurt you. We sat in the bathroom for an hour, him in my lap, no words, just healing. After this, Adam could not walk past me without reaching out to touch me. We had him back.

Early one Saturday morning, Crystal was riding the four-wheeler around the yard. She took a break to go inside and grab a bottle of water. When she came back out, the four-wheeler was not where she left it. She assumed that Adam had taken it for a ride and patiently waited for him to return with it. When Adam came out of the front door, Crystal was really puzzled. As Adam was walking toward her, Crystal asked him where the four-wheeler was. Adam told her that he just got up and hadn't seen it since last night. Just then he noticed behind her in the lake, one handlebar sticking up out of the water. Adam slowly pointed in the direction of the lake. Crystal went white faced.

MY PRINCESS READING HER HOOK AT JASON'S LAKE

Before she had time to fully understand the situation, she heard the front door close and looked up to see Jason come out the front door with a cup of coffee and sit on the swing. From where he sat, he had a direct line of sight to the lake, the handlebar, the four-wheeler. Crystal hurried over to the porch and stood in front of Jason, trying to block his view of the lake. "Hey Jay Jay". This is what she called him when she wanted something. “What’cha been doing? You going anywhere today?”

Jason looked at me with a confused look on his face, like he was a little concerned about Crystal. She finally, in complete panic mode, began to repeat “Don’t look at the lake Jason; Don’t look at the lake. Just look at me.”

This was all I could take. I had held it in as long as I could and finally, I doubled over laughing, I laughed until my ribs hurt. Jason asked what the hell was going on. Adam spilled the beans, proud that for once, Crystal was the one getting in trouble. Jason slowly looked toward the lake and saw the handlebar sticking out of the water. He looked at me and said, “A goddamn seven-thousand-dollar four-wheeler in the lake and you are laughing. By the time he got to the word “laughing” he broke. He was laughing harder than I was. It took the three of us, Adam, Jason, and me to pull it out of the water and what a relief to see it sitting on solid ground again.

During seven years that I attended classes, I commuted between two - and three-hours round trip five days a week. Money was tight and any cash I had went toward gas and the routine of stopping at the Stull’s market on the way to drop the kids off at school. They always went inside and bought a snack to take to school. I would have done anything under the sun to make sure they got this snack.

When all my classes broke for lunch, I generally studied in my car. I took my lunch some days and some days when the refrigerator was beginning to look bare, I left what was there for the kids. Most days this was not a problem. Some days, however, going without lunch was difficult and I came to know every dust particle that hid between and under my car seats. I would search there and in my glove box, under the mats, in the trunk, and in the crease where the back and bottom of the seats meet. All I needed was thirty-five cents to get a bag of chips from the vending machine. This was familiar. Not having food when I was hungry, and I could deal with that. But....When it came to my kids, there is nothing I wouldn't do to make sure they didn't feel that anticipation, that drive, that disappointment, that hunger. Anything.

When I was attending the University of Louisville, I had earned my master's degree and was nearing the end of my course work for my Rank 1 certification in Special Education. I was completing an assignment in the gross anatomy lab when I got a phone call from Jason's stepson who was living with us at the time. I knew this had to be important coming from him. When I answered the phone, he asked me where I was. I told him I was at school in Louisville, which was at least an hour and a half away from home.

He informed me that he had passed the local tavern on the way home. The door was open so he could easily see inside ~~to~~ the bar, and he saw Adam and Crystal ~~were~~ sitting at the bar with their backpacks on their back. Jesus. The response to the next question was so loud and high pitched that he caught the attention of everyone in class. He asked me if I wanted him to go back and pick them up. My level of panic went through the roof and my voice was so high pitched that it sounded like Donald Duck. "Are you kidding me, go get my kids now!" I didn't even ask to be excused I just looked at my professor and said I have to go. I grabbed my bags and ran out the door. I cried the whole way knowing I was going to lose my kids for letting them hang out in bars.

When I got home, I jumped out of my car and ran inside and grabbed both my kids and gave them both the big hug. I could see that both Jason and his stepson were stifling a laugh. I asked Adam what in the world happened that caused them to go to a Tavern. He said Mama we got to Millie's, their babysitter who lives a few yards from the Tavern. She was not home so we walked over to Bob's. When we got inside, he just put us up on the bar stools and gave us a coke. He said we could wait for you to come home.

Adam reassured me, "Mom it's okay. I made sure that I walked on the side by the road and kept my arm around Crystal so she couldn't get run over." It took a few years before I could laugh about this. I can just see my babies sitting on that bar stool with their backpacks on their back, watching the news while patiently waiting for Mama. Thank you, Bob, for taking care of my kids and thank you, Adam for taking care of your sister.

PENIS

Every few weeks I used to visit family in my hometown. On a visit back home to Clarkson, I saw June sitting on her front porch. She waved at me as I drove by. I thought it was odd that she waved so vigorously. My destination was my friend Lana 's house. I was going to visit her and then go back to see June so I could spend time with June without interruption. When I pulled up to Lana 's house, I noticed her car was not in the driveway, but I went up and knocked on the door hoping she was at home, and her husband had gone somewhere in the car. When George answered the door, told me that Lana had gone to the grocery store. I said that I would come back when she returned. He assured me that she would be back any minute and invited me in. Since it would not be long, I decided to go in and wait for her. When I sat down George asked me to come over to the kitchen table and have a cup of coffee. He put on the coffee and left the room.

When he returned to the kitchen, he had changed clothes from a pair of blue jeans to a pair of pajama bottoms. As if that was not odd enough, when he turned around to hand me a cup of coffee, I noticed that the pajamas were split from the fly to the knee. He put the coffee on the table and with his free hand, he reached into his pajamas and took his penis out of his pajamas and just like it was perfectly normal, he casually leaned close to the edge of the table and without expression, placed it on the table. As anyone can imagine, I was so shocked that words would not come out of my mouth. He started a conversation with me with his penis laying on the table!!!

I finally managed to speak, "I think I will go and say hi to June and then I will come back and see Lana when she gets home. He tried to get me to stay, saying Lana would be home very soon. There was no reason to leave and then turn around and come right back. I told him that I was only going to June's. It would be ok. I left his house.

When I got to June's I got out of the car shaking my head. Before I had a chance to say anything to her, she said "I tried to tell you". "What do you mean you tried to tell me?" She responded, "I was waving you down to try to get you to stop." I asked, "So how do you know?" She said, "Because he just did the same thing to me." I was dumbfounded, "Why in the world?" She said, "I don't know what's going on, but somebody needs to tell Lana, and its's not going to be me." I reluctantly volunteered, "I don't have any problem telling her."

When I saw Lana's car pull into the driveway, I went back over and started a conversation with her, "Lana, I know you and George have had a lot of trouble. Are you still in love with him?" Blunt, but I was not practiced in this kind of thing and the last thing I wanted to do was add to the pain I was getting ready to inflict. She turned and looked at me, obviously surprised by my blunt question. "Yes, I love him. Why? What is going on?" I went into detail about what happened while she was away. She seemed to be furious and told me that she was going to have him leave. He had already left the house when she pulled in, but she meant she was going to tell him to get out permanently. I returned to June's house exhausted. George and Lana separated for a brief time and then George moved back home.

June was one of the hardest-working people I knew, yet she had little to show for it. No matter how many hours she put in, she barely managed to cover her basic needs, leaving nothing for indulgences or even simple pleasures. She worked as a server in a busy restaurant, and over time, the long hours and constant demands of the job began to take a toll on her. The physical strain was evident, but even more than that, I could see the emotional exhaustion weighing her down.

As adults, we grew remarkably close, and I spent a lot of time with her. Sometimes, I would stay the night at her house, but more often, we would escape for a night or two in a hotel, giving her a much-needed break from her daily burdens. Those short trips were a way for her to recharge, even if only briefly, before returning to the monotony of daily life. I knew how hard things were for her, so whenever I visited, I made sure to stock up on groceries, easing at least one weight off her shoulders. It was not much in the grand scheme of things, but it was my way of showing her she was not alone. June never asked for help, but I could see the exhaustion in her eyes, and I wanted to do what I could to make her life just a little bit easier. If I could lighten her load, even for a moment, it was worth it.

One weekend we booked a hotel room two hours away from home. The goal was to be far enough away to buffer us against word of any unbecoming behavior making its way back home. The plan was simple: lie by the pool, soak up the sun, and drink like we were twenty-two again. We pulled up to the hotel, lugged in all our "bag," and waited in line to check in. June nudged me in the ribs. I turned to spot a big ugly sign that said, "POOL CLOSED." So, we did the only logical thing. We waited for nightfall, polished off a couple of bottles of Boone's Farm Strawberry Hill and decided, pool closed or not, we were damn well going swimming. The pool fence was at least eight feet tall but that did not deter us. We removed our shoes and with a great deal of moaning and groaning we finally made it over the fence.

With hearts racing, shoes and clothing in a hurried pile, and another wine bottle begging to be opened, we were ready to take the plunge. I dipped my toe into the water, finding the temperature nothing less than perfect. A moment of victory that lasted just short of three seconds. Out of the darkness, a deep male voice shattered the night causing us both to let out a scream. "Ladies, you do realize that you are trespassing, right?" We froze. We were embarrassed and trying desperately to hide our wine bottle. Thank Heaven for the darkness. My mind raced. Security guard? Hotel manager? FBI? CIA? We had no idea who he was, but we knew one thing for sure, we were busted!

Then, with no warning and with much more skill than either of us possessed, he scaled the fence.

Running through my mind were all the prison movies I had ever seen as I looked for his set of handcuffs. He began pulling off his boots, followed by everything else covering his body, except his skin and dove into the water. Not a very smart move. Doesn't he realize we're going to try to escape? June, suddenly much more intrigued than concerned, tilted her head and asked, "So do you work here? "Nope", he said. "My dad owns the place." Then, as if summoned by the devil himself, a voice called out from the darkness. "Hey Son."

JUNE AND ME, AGES 4 AND 3

Horrified, we turned slowly, and there he was! Pops! The owner of the hotel! The keeper of our fate! Standing there, arms crossed, smiling like he had seen this a hundred times before. He gave us a casual wave before turning toward the front doors. Just as we thought we couldn't be more embarrassed, he glanced back one last time and called out, "Don't you girls get wet". June and I scrambled for our clothes, our dignity long gone, and began our painful ascent back over the fence. Still breathless and cursing our wine fueled choice, we heard a sound behind us, a distinct metallic clank. We turned, eyes widening as we watched Daddy's boy stroll to the opposite side of the pool and with a smug little grin, open the unlocked gate. Having narrowly escaped prison, we decided to spend the rest of the night in our room.

For my sixteenth birthday, Linda walked up to the local pharmacy and bought a gift for me. It was a stuffed bear. I couldn't believe Linda saved her money and walked to town to purchase something for my birthday. Noone had ever recognized my birthday. I named my bear Cozy. When Adam was sixteen, I passed Cozy on to Adam for his sixteenth birthday. Adam is forty years old. He has had Cozy for twenty-four years. He sits on the dresser in Adam's bedroom. When Adam was seventeen, Crystal was in her room and a couple of Adam's friends were there waiting for him to get home from work. They had Cozy laying on the bed with them when Adam walked into the room. The first thing he did was in a long-drawn-out way, he said ooooh Cooooozy!!! Everyone in the room burst into laughter and poor Adam realized what he had done. His friends still have not stopped teasing him about that.

I was visiting Adam years later when his young son told me that he wanted a bear like Cozy. Of course, I had to go to town. When I came back, I had a bear for him and gave it to him. Five minutes later Adam came out of the bedroom and said ,"Tell Maw what you named your bear" . Connor looked up at me and said, "I named him Mawzy".

I made it a habit to go and spend weekends at mama's when she was sick. I went and spent a whole week with her when it was getting close to her last days. When I returned home, I checked the answering machine and there was a message from a lady named Elaine. The message was to thank someone in our home for such a nice weekend. Of course, I asked Jason about this, and he totally denied it. He said he knew the lady, but he had not spent the weekend with her and that there was something wrong with her. She was crazy because she had had a head injury. I called her and talked to her about their weekend together, and she gave me a lot of detail and told me that they had flown to Michigan and spent a few nights there and went on to describe all the things they did on the trip. Jason continued to deny going on this trip all the way to the end of our relationship.

June had a son in 2001. I was spending considerable time with June at this time and grew very close with her. Eventually, Dane began visiting Jason and me and spending long weekends. Jason, the kids and I delighted in him. He brought a great deal of joy into our home.

On one of his visits, he was helping me prepare dinner when he jumped down from the counter saying he needed to go to the bathroom. Earlier that day, I had hung a picture over the toilet and had dropped a screw into the bowl. Dane came out of the bathroom and tugged at my shirt," Tammy, something's wrong?". I turned to him and asked, "What is it Dane, are you ok?" His lip started to tremble, and he whispered "Tammy, I think screws is coming' outta me".

Another time, Jason was getting ready to go to work. His truck was parked a good distance from the house at his shop. He remarked something about it being too early for that trek. Dane told him, "Its ok Jason, I will walk you to your truck." He paused for a second and thought about it and finished, "But you will have to walk me back."

When he was about five, he and Jason and I were in the truck when a song came on the radio "Jason's got a girlfriend". Dane interrupted the music quickly to turn to me and say, "Tammy, that's not just a song, Jason really does gots a girlfriend". I responded "Really, what is her name?" "Agnes, you know, she gives Jason beers". This was a server at the local tavern. It was no great surprise. I had suspected it for some time.

My first suspicion came when he bought me a gold necklace for Christmas. A few weeks later, I saw Agnes and she was wearing the same necklace. I complimented her on it and asked where she got it. She stammered a bit and to put her out of her misery, I continued, "I know, he got the same one for me." She was speechless, which was unusual. I let it go, as I have always been one to make sure I have all the evidence before I made an accusation.

It didn't take long. Jason was away for work one week, returning home for the weekend with a suitcase of laundry that I quickly and dutifully began to wash for him. I pulled out a pair of pants and was clearing the pockets when I found a love poem from none other than Agnes. As if that were not enough, a pair of angel earrings were stuffed in a pocket in the suitcase. I took them to him and told him I found my gift. He smiled and started to respond, when I reminded him that Agnes and I were just talking the other day about her collection of angels. I opened his hand and placed them in the palm and closed it and said, "I don't know how you could do this to me." A few days later, he moved out. He allowed the kids and me to stay in the house until I could find something else. He already had an apartment that he shared with Agnes, so it was no imposition for him. After twelve years together, this was not a bad settlement for him.

Two years later, I bought a house in Brandenburg. I moved out and Jason moved back into his house with Agnes. Adam missed the farm, his fishing spot, his hunting cabin, and his four-wheeler. It was heartbreaking to watch his slow decline.

ADAM

By the time Adam was sixteen, school had become a battleground, and he was on the losing side. Day after day, he came home with another failed test, another assignment marked with a glaring red F. His report cards were a sea of them. No matter how much time I spent at the kitchen table with him, trying to help him grasp the material, it never seemed to click. Sitting in a classroom full of kids, Adam became the class clown, trying anything to deflect the shame of not understanding.

ADAM, MY SON AND MY INSPIRATION.

When the laughter faded, the reality remained; he was drowning in failure. One afternoon, he came home and dropped his school bag by the door. He stood there for a moment, his hands shoved deep into the pockets of his jeans, his shoulders stiff with a tension I had never seen before. Finally, he looked at me. His voice was firm, but his eyes showed his lack of confidence.

I'm done with school. I'm going to go work in the log woods.

I looked at him for a long time, weighing my words. I could have fought him on it, demanded he stay in school, and pushed him harder. But Adam had been suffering and forcing him to keep failing seemed like slow torture. "Okay." I spoke. His eyes widened. He hadn't expected that. Maybe he wanted me to argue, to tell him he had no choice. Maybe some part of him hoped I would refuse to let him give up on himself.

But I knew. He wasn't lazy, and he was intelligent. He just wasn't cut out for school. The next day, he started working in the timber business. Some of the older men on the crew took notice, showing him tricks of the trade, teaching him how to navigate the rough terrain, how to work smarter, not just harder. He took to it naturally. It wasn't long before he proved himself, operating and maintaining heavy machinery like he'd been born to do it. Adam was happy. He was flourishing at his new job and his whole attitude changed. But I never had a minute of peace knowing the danger of the work he was doing, the kind of danger that didn't give you time to react. One minute, everything was fine. The next, everything changed.

Before long, when a truck or piece of equipment got stuck in the thick mud, they didn't call the seasoned workers. They called Adam.

It had been raining for days. The ground was thick with mud, sucking at the tires of every machine that tried to cross. Adam was in his skidder, a powerful piece of equipment designed to muscle through just about anything. It was his job to help free any vehicles that got stuck in the mud, and he took pride in it. From a distance, one of his coworkers, an older man named Walt, waved his arms and shouted. The rain muffled his voice, but Adam knew that he was signaling that another truck was stuck. Without hesitation, Adam fired up his skidder and drove toward the immobile vehicle, ready to push it free. Unbeknownst to Adam, the frantic waves of the men standing nearby weren't signals for help. They were warnings. But it was too late.

The truck he had been pushing lurched forward, rolling free from the mud. Only then did Adam see what everyone else had been trying to tell him. The driver of the truck, a man who had taken Adam under his wing, had climbed out and crouched near the front wheel, working on the axle. When the truck moved forward, Adam's friend slipped, falling forward in front of the truck. The massive tire had crushed him. Adam leapt from his skidder, his boots sinking into the mud as he ran forward. His breath came in ragged gasps as he rounded the front of the truck, finding his mentor, his friend lying crushed beneath the weight of the vehicle, his body still, his face frozen in an expression that Adam would never be able to forget.

For weeks after the incident, Adam was unable to sleep. When he did, the image was waiting for him, like a photograph burned into the backs of his eyelids. He couldn't bear to be alone at night. He crowded into bed with his mama, his sister, and his girlfriend, desperate for the comfort of their presence, terrified of closing his eyes and being forced to relive that moment again and again. But fate wasn't finished with him yet. And he was only seventeen.

A few months later, Adam was working with his best friend, a guy he ran around with after hours, someone who had been with him through thick and thin. They were loading a truck; a task they had done countless times before. Once it was full, they needed to secure the load with heavy chains. The routine was simple. One man tossed the chain over the truck bed, the other caught it and locked it into place.

Adam threw the chain. He waited for his friend to secure it, but it didn't move. His stomach twisted. He called his friend's name. No answer. He walked around the truck, his boots heavy against the gravel. The moment he saw his friend lying on the ground, blood pooling beneath his head, he knew. The thick metal hook at the end of the chain had caught him at the crown of his skull. He had died instantly. Adam stood frozen, staring down at his best friend, the weight of it crashing over him like a tidal wave. Another death. Another moment he could never undo. He never talked about it. Not really. Once, in a rare moment of vulnerability, he told me not to bring it up, not to spare his own feelings, but because he didn't want to upset his sister. As if somehow, by burying it deep inside, he could protect the people he loved from the horror of what he had seen and done. But I knew the truth. He carried it every single day. Adam had endured a difficult life. Years of trauma and abuse had led him to start using drugs at just fourteen, a habit that consumed him until he was thirty-five.

One day, I received a call from a friend, her voice heavy with concern. She told me Adam was in terrible shape and feared he would not survive if he did not get help. I called him immediately and told him what I had heard. I followed with a very stern, “I need you to go into inpatient rehab tonight, or you are to forget you know me.” My firmness surprised him, and after a long pause, he replied, “I will Mom.” “I mean tonight, Adam” and he again responded, “I will.” True to his word, that night, he was admitted and has been functionally drug free ever since.

LAYLA’S MIMI AND PAW

CRYSTAL

When Crystal became pregnant at eighteen, it quickly became clear that the baby's father wouldn't be involved. Soon after, she began dating young man who was fully aware of her situation. They continued their relationship throughout her pregnancy. When Crystal was about seven months along, the young man's parents, Teri and Billy, reached out to me. Teri expressed their desire to be involved in the child's life, saying, "I know this is not my place, and you have every right to say no, and we will not be upset. We want to be Mimi and Paw." As usual, I couldn't hold back my emotions. She continued, "I don't have to be Mimi; you could be Mimi. I can a pick something else. "When I was able to calm down, I replied to her, "You're already Mimi."

From that day on, Billy and Teri became grandparents to Layla. Just as I had a wardrobe for her at my house, Teri had one at hers. They even prepared a baby room and were present at the hospital when Layla was born. Teri held her first, and then I did

When Layla was seven, her Mimi died of cancer, it was a terrible time. Billy continued to be one of the best grandpas a little girl could have. This family profoundly affected Layla and helped to shape her into the person she is today. Now, Layla is twenty and when she visits for the holidays, she reminds me, "Maw, you know I can't stay long because I have to go see Paw." And I always tell her, I know you do honey"

Layla spent a great deal of time with her Mimi and Paw, who offered her experiences that I couldn't, like exploring their big farm. Billy took Layla everywhere, and everyone in town knew her. When she was about four, during a trip to Walmart, she got out of the car and said, "Mimi says the Burlington Coat Factory has some awesome deals." I replied, "Well, maybe Mimi will take you to Burlington." She spent a lot of time on Billy's John Deere, and their song was "Big Green Tractor." Little Layla would walk through the house, singing every word to that song. Eventually, things ended between Patrick and Crystal, but I'll always be grateful for the father figure Patrick was to Layla, the love he showed her, and the foundation he laid for her.

Towards the end of her pregnancy Crystal began to have trouble with her blood pressure. When Layla was born, they came home the second night and lived with me. They were home. Crystal kept complaining of a headache. I felt so bad for her. I told her to give Layla to me and go sleep in my bed. Layla and I will lay on the couch because I want to stay awake in case you need me. Layla started crying and I started to get up and get her a bottle when Crystal hollered, and said mama let me do it. I tried to talk to her, but there was no convincing her that she wasn't feeling well, and it was okay for her to let me feed the baby. She came through the hallway into the living room and went into the kitchen. Just a few seconds had passed when I heard a very loud crash. I laid Layla on the couch and ran into the kitchen. Crystal was on the floor, her body convulsing. She was foaming at the mouth, and because her chin was underneath the cabinet, every time her head jerked it would cut deeper into her chin. I tried to move her, but I could not do it. I called 911 and was screaming for them to come and help my daughter, who was on the floor having a seizure. I don't know why she is seizing! Please get here fast.

I begged them. I said please, please, please, please, please, please, please!!!! I'm begging you, get here fast. I don't know what's wrong with her. I don't know. I'm afraid she is going to die. They kept assuring me that they would get there quickly. I called Billy to come get Layla so I could go to the hospital with Crystal in the front of the ambulance. I asked the driver if my daughter was going to die. He said mam we're going to do everything we can to make sure that isn't even a possibility. When we arrived at the hospital, I got out and leaned against the wall, and I just slid down the wall and sat there. The EMT came looking for me and found me sitting there. She took me by both of my hands and said, "She's going to be okay. She is preeclamptic. She is not going to die. The seizures aren't going to continue. It's a one-time thing and she's going to be okay". Crystal spent a night at the hospital and went home the next day. After that she never had any more difficulty.

Dwight

In 2003 I begin a long-distance relationship with a man in Carrolton, Ky. This meant my driving three hours after work on Friday and three hours back on a Sunday every week. After seven years of commuting, I decided to move in with Dwight. He had been asking me to for years. Layla was three years old which made leaving very difficult, For the first three months, I truly thought I would die of grief. I would wash the dishes and stare out the window and cry. My Layla, what had I done?

LAYLA AND HER FAITHFUL COMPANION, MOLLI

Layla visited us often and spent many weekends with us, quickly forming a special bond with Dwight. The two became very close, sharing a love for learning and curiosity about the world. On Saturdays, she would come with us to Dwight's business, where she eagerly found ways to help. Before long, she made it her very own special job to mop the floor, tackling it with excitement and a big smile.

One of Layla's favorite things to do with Dwight was watch documentaries. She was full of questions, and he answered each one with endless patience, always explaining things in a way that made them fun and easy for her to understand. His ability to turn learning into an adventure sparked a deep love for knowledge in her that stayed with her for years.

Layla truly treasured the weekends she and Crystal spent with Dwight. Even long after we separated, she would happily remember those times, speaking fondly of him and the special connection they shared.

One time Crystal and the kids came to spend the weekend with me in Carrollton. Layla kept looking out the window with her hand out as far as she could reach. After a few miles I asked her if she was ok. She said yes, she was ok. After a while I asked her if she wanted to tell me what was wrong. She said, "Do you want me to tell you who I like the most; you or Paw?" Stifling a laugh, I replied, "If you want to tell me." She quickly turned her head toward me, her eyes bugged out and as quickly as a person could say a word, she said, "Paw." As Layla was turning back to the window, I said, "Layla, that's OK." You could just see the weight lift off those seven-year-old shoulders.

Crystal, Layla, Molli, and I decided to have a movie night. We decided to watch "The Wizard of Oz". Layla ended up doing homework. She had to write something about her favorite show, and she chose "The Wizard of Oz". Crystal, Molly, and I were watching TV in the living room. We heard Layla yell out. Can somebody tell me how to spell 'Wizard of Oz". Molly looked at me and their mom and rolled her eyes and yelled back at Layla, "Come on Layla! Sound it out! "Wizzer da boz".

One Sunday, back home in Brandenburg, I was working out in the gym when a friend approached me.

He told me he had seen my “boyfriend” last night at Jim Porter’s night club. Dwight and I had agreed early on that neither of us would go to bars without the other. I knew this could not be Dwight with another woman. Gary said at first, he thought it was me with him, but he soon realized it was not me that Dwight was with but someone who looked a great deal like me. I was not even curious. I replied,” Gary, are you sure it was Dwight? I would be very surprised if he was cheating on me. He just wouldn’t do that to me”.

The next weekend as I was leaving Carrollton, Dwight asked me if I minded going to the grocery store and picking up some sandwich meat and some salads, some chips and a dessert or two. I gladly did this for him and plated it all in preparation for his sons to visit. When I returned the next weekend and went into the bedroom to put my bag away, I noticed that my picture was not in its usual place on the mantle. As I put my things in drawers, I found it face down in one of the drawers. On the way to work the next morning, I noticed my seat was adjusted differently and reaching into the door pocket for a tissue, I found a receipt from a fast-food place for two cups of coffee purchased first thing in the morning. Even more incriminating, I found a sample tube of women’s hand lotion.

Arriving at work, I checked the schedule as I always did and at the border there was a name, number, and date for Tracey. This was outside working hours. Ultimately, placing something in the trashcan, I discovered a stack of ripped paper. It was a Dear John letter to Tracey. At this point, I felt I had to confront

Dwight. He denied everything initially but eventually came forward with the truth.

I had Tracey's number so when we arrived back at the house, I sat on the front porch and called her. He walked out just as she answered the phone, and I asked if I was speaking to Tracey. I did not warn him but simply placed the call. Dwight was right there as I asked her questions about their relationship, and she answered every question without hesitation. She claimed that she did not know he was in a relationship and was shocked to know we had been together for seven years. She commented that there was no sign of a woman in that house. I told her that he had hidden all signs of me before she came. All he could do was sit and listen as I learned the whole ugly truth. At this point, we had been together seven years. I was heartbroken, again, but I cared too much for him to leave.

I continued to work at Dwight's business for a time until I secured a job with a nearby school system. It was there that I met a teacher who was in the process of planning her wedding in Florida. Though we had only known each other for two months, she asked me to be part of her wedding. I was flattered and agreed, deciding to extend the trip to a full week and bring Crystal along with me.

CRYSTAL AND ME IN FLORIDA

While in Florida, away from the routine and weight of my daily life, I found myself reflecting on the state of my relationship with Dwight. The reality of his affair had been something I had endured for as long as I could bear. During that trip, it became painfully clear that I could no longer live with his betrayal. I had always been faithful and put a great deal of effort into our relationship. I was working at his business and on his farm endlessly, remaining loyal and committed to him and our relationship. I couldn't live any longer with the pain, and the daily agony of trying to figure out what I had done wrong. What I had failed to do. At what point did I stop being enough. By the time I returned home, my mind was made up. I told Dwight that I was leaving.

He did what he could to persuade me to stay but words no longer had the power to sway me. I had been deceived too many times by the abuse of words. My mind was made up, and for the first time in a long while, I felt a sense of control over my own life.

When I had first moved in with Dwight, he had purchased a new truck for me, a gesture that, at the time, had seemed generous. But now, as I prepared to leave, he made it clear that the truck was his to keep. He told me to leave it behind. I had spent ten years working tirelessly, every weekend and every summer break while I still lived in Brandenburg, and then every single day after I moved in with him. And yet, after all of that, I walked away with nothing but the clothes I owned. No truck, no money, and no material possessions, just my dignity.

WAYNE

I stayed in the area for another year or so because I could not find a job close to home. I met a guy online and began talking to him long distance. It turned out he lived thirty minutes from Crystal and her children. I explained to him that I planned to move closer to my family once I found a suitable job. We visited each other for a few months and decided to move in together. I moved in with him, since my goal was to eventually be near my family again.

Things started out well. He worked in nearby Louisville and attended the Seminary. He planned to become a minister. I continued to look for a job. Everything was smooth and we got along well for a while.

My sisters and I got together twice a year and spent the weekend together. We would either meet at one of our houses or rent a cabin somewhere. The sister weekend was coming around and I was explaining to him how we had done it since mama died. He teased me, saying he was going with me. I responded playfully, 'No men allowed!"

He did not take this well. "So, a house full of women for the weekend together and their husbands and boyfriends are not allowed"? I clarified that was correct. He told me I was not going. He was furious. He had no intention of letting me go. I had no intention of being told I couldn't. The house my sisters and I stayed in was at least an hour away from where I lived with

Wayne. While there, I walked out with one of my sisters while she smoked a cigarette and saw his car in the parking lot across the street. From that point on, every time we planned a sister event, he would get all out of sorts and talk about it nonstop.

I finally got a job in Hardin County, thirty minutes from where Crystal and Layla lived. I broke it to Wayne that I was moving out. I had seen a house on the way home from my interview. I checked on it and it was vacant. He was upset to say the least, but he had learned it was not easy to stop me once I had made up my mind. I told him I would be moving over the weekend if I was able to get a truck. He replied that it would be foolish when he had a truck. He offered to help me move. I accepted and we began to pack my things. We made two trips back and forth and carried everything into the house. We were able to do this with no animosity. We laughed and talked and worked together to get me all moved in. When we tried to open the door, the key would not work. I called the landlord, and he said he was out of town but added that the back window was not locked as he had painted it the day before. We went around back, and Wayne helped me into the window, and I went around to unlock the door. When we were finished, unloading the second load, he left without incident saying he would be going so that I could get some rest. I put a few things away and decided to lie down.

At that time, I took a sleep aid to help me fall asleep. I had dozed off when I felt the bed move and someone crawled in bed beside me. I screamed, jumped out of bed and switched the light on. It was Wayne. I told him to get out and he told me he knocked and knocked on the door. When I did not answer, he came in through the window. He had driven down the road and his car stalled and would not start. He apologized and said he did not mean to frighten me and did not think I would mind since he had nowhere to go. I was still in a state of panic and insisted he leave.

When he was gone, I left the house to get a pain reliever, and I saw a police officer outside the convenience store. I pulled him aside and relayed to him what had just happened. I asked if they would just keep an eye on my house for few days. I then gave the officer all the identifying information about Wayne that he asked for and went home and back to bed.

Early the next morning, I received a call from Wayne's mom. She asked me what had happened last night. I gave her a short version of the events and asked why she was calling. She told me that Wayne had been watching TV with a friend the night before when armed officers broke his door down, held a gun to his face, handcuffed and arrested him. He was charged with burglary and sexual assault and was facing ten years in prison. I was horrified. I explained to her that I had taken a sleep aid that can make me very confused if awakened abruptly.

I assured her I had no intention of his being arrested and that I would do everything in my power to get him out of this. I set about to do so. I spoke with the officer I had seen the night before and he was as shocked as

I was to learn that Wayne had been arrested. He had spoken to his superior about it and warned me that he a stickler for the law.

I made an appointment to speak with him and learned that he had taken in upon himself to pursue the case. He let me know that he ran a taut ship, and these things do not happen in his town. I told him I wanted to drop the charges, and he responded that it was out of my hands. I let his mother know what I had learned and reassured her that I was not finished. I wrote a letter to the judge, the county attorney, the prosecutor, the initial officer, the police chief and Wayne's attorney and explained exactly what happened and that there was no burglary and no sexual assault. The case was dropped. The seminary would not allow Wayne back on campus even after the charges were dropped.

TEETH

This story has been the hardest one for me to tell. In fact, I kept it locked away for decades tucked in that quiet place where we put things too painful to speak aloud. It wasn't something I ever imagined sharing, not with friends, not with family, and certainly not in writing. When I started working on this book something shifted. I felt the need to be honest, not just about the things that happened to me but about the way they shaped me and the way I adapted, survived, and eventually began to heal. That's when I first shared this secret with Mary.

At the time Mary had been visiting me every weekend after my health had taken a bad turn and I could no longer take care of myself the way I once had. She became a steady presence in my life, one of the few. She brought groceries, helped me around the house, and just sat with me and reminded me that I wasn't alone. On one of those visits, just as she was getting ready to head home, she paused, sat back on the sofa, and said something I'll never forget. Hey Tammy, she said her voice gentle but firm. I want you to include the story about your teeth in the book. I didn't answer right away. My first instinct was to say no to protect that small, scared part of myself that still enveloped me in shame every time I thought about it. But the way she asked, without judgment and with real care, made me pause. She wasn't just asking for the sake of the book; she was asking because she knew the power of stories. She knew that sometimes the things we're most afraid to share are the very things that can both bring healing and help someone else feel less alone.

If my story could lessen someone else's shame, someone else's fear, even just one person, then maybe it was worth the discomfort of telling it. I finally decided that it was time. So here it is.

I lost several of my teeth due to domestic violence. Romey hit me in the face more than once and some of those blows left permanent damage not just to my mouth but to my sense of self-worth. Of all the things I endured during that time, the damage to my teeth was strangely one of the hardest to carry. It sounds simple, maybe even superficial and vain, but it wasn't. It was about more than appearance. It was about identity, dignity and my barely existent self-confidence, which was grossly diminished the first time I lost a tooth.

I was in shock. I remember standing in the bathroom looking in the mirror not able to fully comprehend what just happened. I held the tooth in my hand like it was a piece of myself that had broken off and couldn't be put back. I couldn't just throw it away so I wrapped it in a tissue and tucked it away in the back of a drawer, as if keeping it might somehow make things feel less final. It was the mid 1980s and the possibility of getting it fixed was out of the question. I didn't have the money, and I didn't have the confidence to walk into a dentist office to ask for help. The odds of getting it fixed were about as likely as winning the lottery and bumping into Tom Petty on the same day. In other words, impossible.

But I've always been stubborn, and I've never been one to give up completely. Even when things seem hopeless, I'd find some way to keep going. So, I tucked my tooth away and stopped smiling. I learned to talk with my hand over my mouth and became an expert in avoiding photographs. Eating in front of others became a quiet kind of torture. I would cut up burgers and hot dogs and sandwiches so I would never have to bite into anything and risk someone seeing the gap. As time went on the shame grew. It followed me everywhere and was present in every interaction. It was like carrying around a secret, only it wasn't invisible. It was right there on my face. I became obsessed with hiding it, terrified of what people might think if they saw the empty place where a tooth should be.

One day, out of pure desperation, I bought a tube of super glue. I knew it wasn't meant for anything like this, but I didn't care. I held a saved tooth in my hand, applied the glue, and pressed it carefully to my gums. To my surprise it stayed in place; not forever but long enough. Sometimes for a day or two, giving me just enough time to get through whatever social event or outing I needed to attend. I started carrying super glue with me everywhere. I never left a room without it. It became a lifeline.

At one point I was in a long-term relationship for twelve years and for the entire time I never told my partner. Every time we went out to eat, I made sure to hide the glue somewhere, in my bra, my shoe, or my purse. If we were at a restaurant and the tooth came loose, I'd excuse myself, rush to the bathroom, and glue it back. I got so good at it that no one ever suspected a thing but sometimes I wondered if my partner thought I was secretly sniffing glue.

The truth is it wasn't just about the violence. I was used to that. It was about the shame, and I was just fed up worrying about the possibility of a tooth falling out before I could get a chance to fix it. The bigger issue was my fear, not the fear of pain and not the fear of needles. What I couldn't handle was the shame of the condescending looks and the cruel remarks of those who didn't bother to hide their disgust. Too many times I had sat in a dentist chair and been made to feel small, like my worth was measured by the state of my mouth.

My best friend at the time eventually had enough. She told me that I was going to the dentist, like it or not. I'll go with you; sit beside you and hold your hand. I'll even let you sit on my lap if that's what it takes. but you are going. And she meant it. After enough convincing I agreed to go. I really did try, but as soon as I sat in the chair my body betrayed me. My chest tightened I couldn't breathe. I bolted out the door and into the car leaving my friend behind. It took me three years before I had the courage to try again.

Eventually I found a university dental school that did dental work at a reduced price to help with the education of students studying dentistry. It seemed like a safe place to start, more low key and more affordable.

A young technician came in and did a preliminary exam then left to get his instructor. When the instructor walked in, he took one look, jabbed at my tooth with a sharp instrument, frowned, and without a trace of compassion, said, "I don't know what the hell that is." and walked away. I was done, embarrassed, crushed. I turned to the tech and asked if his instructor was just having a bad day or is he always an asshole. The technician shrugged, "He's always like that." and just like before I walked out. By the time I reached my car I was crying. Still, I knew I had to find a solution.

I started researching home denture kits. I spent years reading reviews, watching videos, and saving money. When I finally bought one, I studied the instructions like a sacred animal. I worked on those dentures for hours and when I finally finished and placed them in my mouth, I walked to the mirror and looked at myself. I dropped to my knees, pressed my face to the floor, and cried. Not from sadness. but from the overwhelming relief of seeing myself again. Those homemade dentures got me through a tough time, but they were not a permanent solution. My remaining teeth kept getting infected and the pain became unbearable.

One day I saw an ad for a place called Affordable Dentures. I looked at it and read everything I could. I found a biography for one of the dentists. There was something different about him. Some of the words in his biography made me feel like, just maybe, I could trust him. I made an appointment with him. I was shaking in the chair when he walked into the room, and when he tried to reassure me about the injection and the procedure, I told him I was not afraid of the shots. He asked me what I was afraid of. “I'm scared of you.”, I said. He looked at me; truly looked at me and asked why I was afraid of him. I said, “Because I'm afraid of what you might say.” He didn't laugh and he didn't scold me. He just smiled and said, “Well, here's what I'm going to say. We're going to get you new teeth.” Right then and there I broke down and cried in that chair like a child. He patted me on the shoulder and said,” I know you have been through a lot, but you don't have to go through it anymore.” He pulled my remaining teeth that day and fitted me with a temporary set of false teeth. Three weeks later I had permanent teeth and for the first time in years I smiled without fear.

There is a special place in the world for people like him, people who are sensitive to the pain in others, and respond with kindness, by treating you like a person and not a problem. There is also a place for those who make things harder, who leave scars, instead of helping to heal.

I think about the long journey it took to get where I am now, the shame, the fear, and the pain. But I also think about the strength it took to keep going, to fight for something better. Now when I smile, I really smile. It's not just about teeth, it's about freedom, it's about reclaiming something I thought I'd lost forever.

PINK SLIP

The day I decided to apply for my first job remains vividly in my mind. I was nervous but determined to take that step toward independence. The hardest part was not the idea of ~~actually~~ working; it was figuring out how to present myself on paper. At the time, I did not have a clue where to begin with a resume. Thankfully, I had a family friend, Mrs. Peterson, who offered to help me out. She was the go-to person in the neighborhood for anything remotely professional, and I figured if anyone could make me look like a great candidate, it would be her.

I talked to Mrs. Peterson about my dilemma, and she invited me over one afternoon with a notebook and pen. "We're going to figure this out," she said with a smile. She asked me about my schooling, any activities I had participated in, and, most importantly, what skills I could bring to a job. I hesitated, realizing I did not have much formal experience to share. I mumbled something about babysitting my younger siblings and doing chores around the house, but nothing seemed impressive enough to me. Mrs. Peterson, however, had a knack for turning the most mundane tasks into valuable skills. "Let me ask you this," she said. "What is something you have done that made you proud? Something you think you are really good at." I thought for a moment and then said, almost without thinking, "Last Thanksgiving, I made dinner for the whole family." Her face lit up. "That's perfect!" she exclaimed, scribbling something down in her notebook.

I did not think much of it until she handed me the finished resume a couple of days later. She had typed it up beautifully, with clean lines and professional wording. But when I read it, I could not help but laugh. Under "Skills," she had written: Excellent at organizing and preparing a full Thanksgiving dinner for extended family. At first, I was mortified. I thought, who is going to hire someone because they can cook a turkey? But Mrs. Peterson stood by her decision. "Listen," she said, "This is not just about cooking. You are telling them you can manage a big project, juggle multiple tasks, work under pressure, and meet deadlines. Plus, it is memorable! They will read that and want to learn more. "I decided to trust her judgment and sent out the resume as it was.

A week later, I got a call for an interview at a small café. When I walked in, the manager smiled and said, "I must admit, the part about Thanksgiving dinner caught my eye. Tell me more about that." We ended up talking for most of the interview about how I coordinated dishes, managed timing, and even solved a last-minute crisis when the stuffing did not turn out as planned. By the end, she told me I had the job. Looking back, I realize Mrs. Peterson was teaching me an important lesson: it is not just about what you have done, but how you present it. That quirky little detail about Thanksgiving dinner gave me the confidence to tell my story, and it landed me my first job. It is a reminder that sometimes, the things we overlook in ourselves are exactly what make us. I was proud to have gotten the first job that I applied for. I eventually went to school and became a teacher, with a specialty in speech therapy.

My final year of teaching was in 2012 after several relocations over the years. On the surface it felt like a good move. It was in Hardin County, which was close to the school where I'd been hired and more importantly near my children and grandchildren. I had every reason to believe this would be a fresh solid start. I'd been teaching special Education for seventeen years and while the job came with some challenges, I loved the work and I loved the students. I had no reason to think that this year would be any different.

Two days into the school year the principal called me into her office. I thought it was probably a routine welcome or some basic housekeeping. Instead with a certain glib satisfaction in his voice he informed me that I was no longer considered tenured. Apparently when a teacher moves between Kentucky counties, a one-year probationary period is required before tenure can be reinstated. He told me that I had failed to complete that probationary year. During a previous district change there was an oversight that he seemed to be eager to correct. The message beneath his words were clear. My security was gone and he intended to keep it that way.

That conversation marked the beginning of a slow calculated unraveling of my teaching career from that point forward. I was no longer treated as a professional with nearly two decades of experience. I was a burden and an outsider. Someone being quietly pushed toward the door on my first official day. He escorted me to my workplace. It was a single desk placed across the room from the school's other two speech therapists. My desk was completely bare, no pencils, no paper, no materials of any kind. It was clear from the outset that I was not expected to feel at home. I was not part of the team and I was not accepted. Trying to make the best of the situation, I approached the principal and asked if there was a supply cabinet where I could find some basic supplies like tape, pencils, the usual tools to do my job. He told me I would have to purchase my supplies on my own. Then he added almost as a joke that the school counselor might be willing to loan me a roll of tape but I would need to return it at the end of the day. I asked if I could use my lunch break to go to Walmart and pick up what I needed from the store. He gave me a sharp look and said, " I don't know what you did at your last school but here we come to work, not to go shopping." Just as he finished this tirade, the two other speech therapists walked through the door with Walmart bags and McDonald's drinks in their hands. He didn't flinch! He just moved on as if nothing was out of place.

The second week of school, he called me into his office again. He said he had been told I had only completed sixteen speech screenings. I explained that there were thirty-two total screenings and with three therapists we were supposed to split the workload evenly, which was about eleven screenings each. I had done sixteen, which was more than my share. He showed me a piece of paper where he had written 320 screenings. According to his version of the math, I had left 304 screenings for the other therapists to complete. I tried to correct him, but he didn't want clarification; he wanted justification. He closed the meeting by accusing me of not being a team player and of nitpicking over the number of evaluations he recorded. I told him that I did not consider it nitpicking because this was putting my job at risk. He was not happy at this point.

I contacted the director of special education and asked to be transferred to another school which she quickly put in motion. At the second school my middle of the year evaluation was completed by the principal and the results were much the same as evaluations I had received over the last seventeen years. No negative remarks. Only positive remarks across the board. I felt like the issue was resolved and I would not have to be concerned about my year end evaluation.

I was wrong! About a month before the end of the school year I was contacted by the director of special education telling me that the principal of the initial school was asking to have me back. He had contacted her and told her that he needed another speech therapist. I returned to the school for three weeks and then sat through an evaluation with the principal for the second time. When I received the paperwork, the initial count for my screenings had not been changed. At the end of the evaluation was the recommendation not to rehire. Twelve years later I still have a box containing my evaluations from seventeen years, with Hardin County on top. I keep those ~~in order~~ to look back on the seventeen years of glowing remarks and recommendations to rehire. I did that to reassure myself that what this one principal at this one school decided was the quality of my work was false.

The rest of the year followed the same pattern, hostile and dismissive. No matter what I did it was never enough. The coldness and isolation were relentless all the way to the last day of school when he handed me a pink slip. In Kentucky at that time, an informal dismissal like that can make it almost impossible to get another job. In other districts most principals would at least offer the courtesy of letting the teacher quietly seek another position in the district. But not him. He made it official. There was one other teacher who wasn't returning the next year, but she did not get a pink slip.

At the year-end staff meeting, the Principal stood before the group he announced that two of us would not returning next year. He was smiling as if he were announcing a retirement party. He told everyone that he had bought a card for each of us and the entire staff had signed them to show their appreciation. At lunch I returned to my room and opened the card. To my surprise, found it was completely blank! No notes, no signature, not a single word. I sat with my head in my hands for a long time just staring into the silence inside that card. It said everything I needed to know.

I did not go back to the meeting after lunch. I picked up the boxes I had already packed and walked out of the building and didn't look back. Seventeen years of students whose names and faces I still remember. And over seventy formal evaluations, none of them with a single negative remark. I was walking away from this school with a pink slip in my hand and with no way to challenge the falsehood used to justify it. I still believe that principal had decided my fate the moment I walked through the door; and I still believe he made sure the year ended exactly the way he planned it.

After I lost my teaching job, I packed up what little I had and moved to Louisville hoping to put some distance between myself and the mess I had just left behind. I found work that was not exactly what I wanted, but it kept my mind occupied. Most nights after work I ended up at the neighborhood bar. It was big, loud and sprawling and easy to get lost in if you weren't paying attention. I liked the anonymity of it. No one cared who you were or why you were there and that suited me just fine.

Not long after I settled into my seat and ordered a drink, a man I didn't recognize slid into the stool beside me. He leaned in and offered to buy me a drink. I declined politely but firmly. I learned that sometimes accepting a drink came with expectations that I wasn't interested in fulfilling. He didn't take the hint. He stayed there and was making occasional small talk, bits of meaningless chatter that made my head spin. I responded here and there but mostly I was hoping he would get bored and move on. When I went out it was to quiet the noise in my head; to breathe in a space where nobody needed anything from me, and a lengthy conversation with a stranger wasn't just unappealing. It felt like work. The next thing I remember was waking up ~~in the~~ in a dark room. I had no idea where I was or how I got there. I could feel someone beside me, but I could see nothing.

I was afraid to move for fear of waking the person lying asleep beside me. I had a tremendous headache that started pounding when I attempted to get out of bed. I was disoriented and confused and shocked to learn I had no clothes on. As my eyes began to adjust to the darkness, I could make out three windows, each covered by black garbage bags. My God, where am I. I began to make my way along the walls making sure not to turn anything over until I reached a door. My heart pounding, I slowly turned the knob. To my great surprise, the door opened but all I found was more darkness. Again, feeling for doors, I traced my hand along the wall until I found a second door. My panic was quickly rising as I opened the next door. It was a bathroom, I searched for a switch and hoped that I would find my clothing.

I began to frantically open the bathroom drawers looking for anything I could use as a weapon. When I opened the drawers, each one contained sets of false teeth that looked as if black hair dye had been splashed over them. I grabbed for the door and took off down a long hall until I found another door. My panic was full blown when I found it locked. When I was able to regain my composure, it registered that it was locked on my side.

I unlocked the door, and opened it, all the while praying that I had found a way out when I saw a light. I was at the top of a stairway which brought on flashbacks of coming into the room last night. I ran down the stairs toward the door and grabbed a blanket off a sofa as I went out. I ran to a neighbor and pounded on the door. An older gentleman answered the door and did not even ask any questions as I asked to use a phone. I called a friend to pick me up. I was too embarrassed to call one of my sisters this time.

Not long after this happened, I was at the same bar. I was leaning against the wall, listening to the band. A guy probably ten years younger than me walked up beside me and put his drink in the window. He was drinking a beer. I was drinking a vodka tonic. After he finished his beer, he headed to the bar asking if I wanted a drink. I knew better than to go there. When he came back, he changed his drink from beer to vodka tonic.

We both had a drink sitting in the window and after I finished mine, I went to the bar for another. As soon as I started across the floor I stumbled. The room started spinning, and I felt nauseous. My head was pounding. The bartender, one that I knew very well, ran out from behind a bar and came out and put his arm on my waist. He walked me over to the bar and sat me down on a barstool. He said do you even know what that son of a bitch did? He proceeded to help me up onto a barstool. Then he started towards this young man who darted out the door. He told me that he had put something in my drink. He said I have been seeing you ~~come~~ here for ten years, and I've never seen you like this. He continued, “I get off at midnight and you are going to sit on that barstool drinking coffee until then”. When I get off work, I will tell you if you are safe to drive home. After an hour or so I told him that I felt okay, and he released me to drive home to nurse my headache.

MY "BOSS"

My first job after leaving the school system was at a facility in Louisville, Kentucky working with individuals with intellectual disabilities. I did not know anything about working with this population, but I knew it was a job. I put in an application and a few days later, I got a call from a man named Jim who wanted me to meet for lunch to conduct an interview and tell me more about the position. I was hired on the spot and began work the next week. After two years there, the state took over the facility and I took another job working with the same population.

This job was quite different from my previous job. I found the staff to be distant and territorial. It felt as though new hires were under a microscope and the aim was not to retain staff but to find a reason to get rid of them. The job was very demanding, and I was out of my comfort zone. One day I was asked to do a swallowing evaluation for an elderly gentleman who coughed constantly when he ate. I completed the evaluation. Based on the evaluation results my recommendation was that he continue to eat by mouth rather than placing a feeding tube.

This meeting happened the day before we left for Thanksgiving break. I was speaking in front of the doctor, the nurse practitioner, the nurse, the occupational therapist, and physical therapist. They decided to go against my recommendations, which was typical. After today he would no longer be eating, and they would insert a tube for him to receive nutrition.

As we left the room, and everyone was walking out talking about Thanksgiving and what they're going to have for their meal. I picked up my books and my purse, and as they were walking away, I slammed my fist on the table, just as hard as I could, and said, “You all make me sick”. I said if this were a movie, you would all be crying about the end and how this poor old man who is getting ready to get this terrible news on Thanksgiving weekend. He will not be getting his Thanksgiving meal.

I returned to my office. A few minutes later I got called from my boss’s office. She told me she was very upset with me. She said, “I have half a mind to let you go.” She continued “You made Sarah cry”. I told her she may want to fire everybody in the department because you can’t imagine the times they've made me cry.” I walked back to my office, put my jacket on and packed up my personal belongings. I put my briefcase over my shoulder and started out the door.

I was about halfway between my office and the front door when I got a call from Jim. He said, “Well, Tammy they did it. They are letting you go.” I responded, “They are not letting me go. I do not work here anymore. I'm walking out the door as I speak.” Just a couple minutes later I got another phone call from Jim. “Hey Tammy, your boss asked me to tell you to bring the key and your badge to her office.” I said, “Jim, tell her that if she can get off her butt and walk fast enough to catch me, she can come get the badge. I still have the badge.

Jim told me to come to his current workplace, Lee Specialty Clinic, in the morning. He wanted to discuss a position that he had been preparing for me to fill. Lee Specialty Clinic was an interdisciplinary clinic for individuals with intellectual and developmental disabilities. I was excited and honored by the opportunity to be a part of the team there. My experience at Lee was highly rewarding. The patients I encountered there were some of the most memorable and delightful of my thirty-year career. The patients were not the only source of joy that I encountered at this job. I met Sarah.

Sarah was an occupational therapist at Lee Specialty Clinic. We were in a unique position that allowed us to collaborate to treat our clients. We did magical things together. We made gains with clients that would never have happened had we worked alone. We loved the tough ones that everyone else was afraid to take on.

Sarah and I were the dream team at work. Outside of work, we were an accident waiting to happen. We looked for trouble and we found it. We laughed at everything. We took care of one another, and we loved one another.

We were out one night when we walked past this young man who made a rude remark about a certain part of Sarah's anatomy. He was probably six and a half feet tall. I was behind Sarah, so I heard the remark, but she did not. I stopped with the intention of poking him in the chest. I tried to stand on my tip toes but I still couldn't reach him so I jumped, poked him in the chest, and in a voice that I hoped would leave him shaking in his boots, said, "Hey tall boy. You do not disrespect my friend". He stood like a statue. And laughed at me.

Relationships and jobs and responsibilities changed, and Sarah and I drifted apart. Every now and again one of us would miss the other and we would make contact. I spoke with her one day to learn she had moved from the house that we had so many fun nights in. I asked where she moved to, and she gave me the address. She was a half mile from my new home. We continued to talk for a bit and swore we would get together soon. As we were ending the call, I told her if I never saw her again, it was a comfort to me to know I could look at the hill as I'm turning toward my driveway and know she is up there.

I ended up leaving Lee Clinic because of a major conflict between me and another speech therapist that was beginning to negatively impact patient care. I accepted a position at Kaleidoscope, an adult day health center.

Kaleidoscope was a wonderful place to work. The team of therapists were some of the best and most enjoyable I had had worked with. The individuals attending the center were treated with kindness and respect and received the best of care. My tenure at Kaleidoscope was enjoyable and I thought I might finish out my career there. However, I received a call from a familiar voice offering another work opportunity. I couldn't refuse.

While I was finishing paperwork, Jim called asking about my current job. I informed him that everything was going well and expressed my satisfaction with my position at Kaleidoscope. He inquired further about my level of satisfaction and mentioned, "I have something going on and would like to involve you." I was intrigued and excited to hear what he had on his mind. I responded, "Well tell me what you've got. You are a hard man to say no to." I had always felt a sense of security working under Jim. Quite simply, I trusted Jim unconditionally.

He described a plan to take his current business and move it to a much larger building. He wanted me to get ahead of the move and get the therapy department up and running before the other therapists arrived. I hesitated for two seconds and told him to give me a start date. He really was a hard man to say no to, and I owed him more than I could ever repay.

After about a year of working at this job and preparing the speech department to transition, the move was initiated. I was soon sharing my large work area with occupational therapy. What an experience that turned out to be. We had a blast working and playing together. The speech therapists were owners and administrators and occupied offices in a different part of the building. This was the beginning of my seven years with Mariposa and the best years of my professional life.

Jim was one of the owners of Mariposa. The other two owners were fair and kind and went above and beyond to make the workplace a safe and pleasant one. My clients were my joy, and I could not wait for Monday to roll around so I could get back to work. Everyone worked well together and for the clients. It was my second home, and my second family met me there every morning. I thanked God every morning for my job.

When I first started working at Mariposa, I was welcomed with open arms by a team that exuded warmth, professionalism, and camaraderie. Among the many wonderful people I met, two individuals stood out—Will and Tiffany. Their kindness, support, and unwavering friendship became a cornerstone of my experience at Mariposa. We often had humorous moments that we chose not to share with the broader group.

Together, Will and Tiffany complemented each other in ways that were inspiring. Their friendship with me flourished, built on mutual respect, shared experiences, and an abundance of humor. The bond we formed was unbreakable and treasured.

Our friendship took on an even deeper meaning when my granddaughter, Molli, ~~made an important decision. Molli~~ confided in me on the way to work one morning that she wanted to be baptized. She had decided to ask Will and Tiffany to be her Godparents.

The choice was a testament to the profound impact Will and Tiffany had on our lives. They had become more than friends. They were family. Molli's request was met with overwhelming acceptance.

Since that day, our bond has only strengthened. Will and Tiffany's roles as Molli's Godparents have been marked by their unwavering support, guidance, and love. They have embraced this responsibility with open hearts, continuing to be a positive and nurturing presence in her life.

As I reflect on my time at Mariposa, I am filled with gratitude for the friendships that have shaped my path. The journey was not just about the work we accomplished but about the connections we forged and the family we created together. Will and Tiffany's friendship is a precious gem in my life, and I am thankful every day for the blessings they have been to Molli.

My Honey

I was fifty-four years old and had been single for some time when one night I decided to get out of the house and go listen to some live music. I did an internet search and found Captain's Quarters, a bar and restaurant on the banks of the Ohio river. A glass of wine overlooking the river in Louisville, Kentucky sounded like just what I needed.

When I walked into the grill, I noticed double doors that led to a patio and wooden deck that, as advertised, provided a breathtaking view of the river. I could hear live music coming from somewhere beyond the doors. I walked outside and started up the steps to the deck when I spotted him. Sitting at the end of the bar, back to the river, wearing sunglasses and a yellow cap, he was having a glass of red wine. I stood for a second checking him out until I noticed he was staring back at me. I quickly made my way to the other end of the bar where the band was set up and spoke with the sound mixer. The deck had four large round posts in front of the bar with barely room to get past them when the bar stools were disheveled. I looked up just in time to see "yellow hat" holding onto one of the posts and looking around it, right at me. I continued ~~to~~ talking to the sound guy and watching out of the corner of my eye as the guy made his way closer and closer, partly hidden by the large posts. I pretended not to notice and continued listening to the sound man. As suddenly as he appeared around that first post he was gone. I had had my fill and was ready to go home. But I wasn't finished with "yellow hat"

The next night I returned to Captain's Quarters with one purpose in mind. The whole drive over, I was hoping that he would be there. On arrival, I went directly to the deck and looked toward the end of the bar and there he was. He was sitting at the end of the bar, back to the river, again in sunglasses and a yellow cap. Once again, he was having a glass of red wine. He and another gentleman were at the barstools at joining corners. I tried to play it cool and sat next to the other gentleman hoping he would eventually leave, pass out, or die. I sat for a good thirty minutes, listening to their conversation, getting a particularly good impression of "Yellow Hat".

Finally, third wheel left and yellow hat asked if he could buy me a glass of wine. I barely looked at him and responded, "Sure". When the wine came, he offered it to me, and I pointed to the bar and spoke. "Just set it here." He asked me to move to the next bar stool, the one next to him. "I am here to listen to the band." I responded. We had exchanged a few niceties when he asked again. "Why don't you move down here. I am having trouble hearing you." He was pointing to the seat vacated by his friend. I moved down but kept my back to him.

He offered me a second glass of wine and asked if I wanted to move to the sectional on the deck and I agreed that it would be more comfortable. Halfway through my second glass of wine, he said something that made me laugh and I leaned toward him briefly putting my head on his shoulder. We spent another few minutes together talking when I told him I thought it was time for me to go home. He offered to drive me home. I had taken a taxi from home to Captains Quarters, because I knew I would be drinking. I accepted, trying not to show my excitement. I invited him in for one last glass of wine, but he declined. He asked if he could call me, and I gave him my phone number. I thanked him for the ride, and he headed home.

He soon called and we arranged our first real date. When he arrived, I was drinking wine out of a coffee cup to make it less obvious to law enforcement. He asked me what I was drinking, and I said it was red wine. He asked me if I liked red wine and I replied, "I don't like any of it. I just like the buzz." He laughed and replied 'Well, you're in the right car." He took me to a wonderful wine bar. This time when I invited him inside, he accepted my invitation.

On our second date, we headed back to Captain's Quarters. On the way, my phone rang. It was my daughter. She asked, "Mom, are you alone?" I told her no; I was with a friend. She paused, and I could feel my heart pounding. Finally, she said, "Chris is dead." I let out a quiet scream and asked what had happened. She told me he had killed himself—hung himself, to be exact. She paused again and then said, "Mom, he hung himself in your tree." That hit me like a ton of bricks. There was one tree in the yard at the house we had lived in before. He had helped me build an eight-by-eight sandbox for the kids under that tree. We hauled load after load of sand, so they would have a clean place to play. And now, years later, he hung himself from the only limb on the only tree in the yard.

I remember the phone slipping out of my hand onto the floor. Jeff looked over at me and asked if I was okay. All I could say was, "My friend just hung himself." He said, "Oh my God, that is terrible. Are you sure you are okay?" I told him I was fine. He offered to drive me home and reschedule our date, but I repeated that I was fine.

As we continued the drive to the restaurant my mind jumped from one scene to the next; the terrible winter storm; Chris lived about a quarter mile from us; such a good friend to us; coming over to dinner; helping entertain the kids so I could have a break. He was too kind for this world, the tree where we built the sandbox. These things kept playing over and over in my mind.

During a snowstorm, we had no electricity. We blocked off most of the rooms in the house with sheets and blankets to conserve heat, keeping just one room warm with a propane heater. I was worried about the pipes bursting, and though we had a wood stove, we did not have any wood, and with the roads completely buried in snow, no one could get to us. But Chris found a way. He walked through waist-deep snow from his house to ours, carrying armloads of firewood so we could keep the stove going. He did this over and over until the electricity was restored.

When we arrived at the restaurant, Jeff ordered me a glass of wine. After drinking it, I got up to grab another. As I walked across the room, I saw something—a black streak in the sky—and I heard a voice ask, "Isn't this what you've always wanted?" I felt like the voice was referencing how I had always dreamed of living near the river. I sat back down with the wine, and as I did, a man walked onto the deck. He locked eyes with me and stared at me the entire way across the floor until he sat down. That same voice came again, saying, "That is the devil, and he hates you." What happened next was completely unlike me. I leaned over to Jeff, put my hand up his shorts, touched him, and said, "Take me home. I want to fuck your brains out." I have never said anything like that in my life. Not because I am too proper, but because it is just not something I would say.

Unfortunately, Jeff's friends were standing nearby and heard every word. Jeff quickly stood up and said, "I think it's time to take her home." When we got back to my place, I asked him to stay the night because I was scared, and he kindly agreed. At some point, I called my best friend, rambling about what she later told me was nonsense. She told me she had no idea what I was talking about but warned Jeff, a man she had never met before, not to leave me alone.

The next morning, I woke up, and Jeff was gone. I felt terrified. I called my friend Sarah and told her I had done something horrible the night before, but I could not remember what. I just had this awful feeling. I tried calling Jeff all morning, but he did not answer. Finally, I asked Sarah to reach out to him and explain that I was not crazy or on drugs. I must have been in shock and could not remember anything. Later, Jeff called and told me what had happened. Once he realized I wasn't strung out or anything like that, he asked me out again.

But I told him I could not. I was too mortified by my behavior.

A few weeks passed, and he called again. This time, I told him he had talked me into it. I called Sarah and told her, “You’re going to think I’m crazy, but I’m going out with Jeff again.” She told me I might want to reconsider and insisted that I stop by her house. When I got to Sarah’s house, she showed me her phone. The night before, she had been out dancing at Jeff’s hangout and saw him there.

Later that night, she received a text that read, “ I sure do like your moves, I would like to take you out for a glass of wine sometime.” I told Sarah that I did not know Jeff that well, but I still did not think that was language that Jeff was use.

I called Jeff, and the moment he answered, I tore into him. “Really? You’re hitting on my best friend the night before you ask me out?" Jeff sounded completely baffled. “What are you talking about?” I read the text to him, my voice dripping with accusation. There was a brief silence before he responded, his tone flat and irritated. “That’s not me.” I wasn’t as gullible as he seemed to think. “It is your number. Sarah, has it saved under your name, Tammy’s guy”.

His voice revealed his growing impatience. “It’s not me, what is the phone number?” I checked the number on my phone and asked her the number her text came from. When she told me, my eyes widened, and I was about to tell Sarah that it was not him, but she had already caught on. Immediately her lip started quivering. Within seconds, she was in tears. Between sobs, she managed to choke out, “I’ve ruined your chance with Jeff!” Between the quivering lip and the drama of this statement, I burst out laughing. I laughed so hard that I rolled off the couch, clutching my stomach to just tolerate the pain.

Meanwhile, poor Jeff was still on the phone, pacing the floor at work. I finally pulled myself together long enough to say, “I’m sorry. We figured out you didn’t do it.” Without missing a beat, he shot back, “No shit. I’ve been telling you that. I gotta go.” He hung up on me, which sent me into another fit of laughter, leaving me once again rolling on the floor in agony over the pain of laughing so hard. I finally recovered from laughing and Sarah recovered from crying, and we began problem-solving what we were going to do about poor Jeff.

After Jeff and I had been dating for a while and we both felt comfortable with the idea, we invited Layla and Molli over to my place for dinner. We drove to Crystal’s house to pick them up. When we arrived at my apartment, I couldn’t find my key, so I asked Jeff to use his. The girls looked at each other wide eyed and Molli commented in a long drawn out, “Awkward”. Layla responded with an uncomfortable and quick ‘That’s not creepy at all!” After dinner, not really knowing what to do with them, we decided to take them to the park where we spent most of the evening swinging and, of course, taking photos.

LAYLA, MOLLI, AND ME AT THE PARK

Jeff and I started out in a cozy one-bedroom condo, but with my grandkids visiting frequently, we soon realized we needed more space. That realization led us to search for a larger home, and we were fortunate to find a three-bedroom townhouse in the same complex. It was the perfect upgrade, not just for the extra room, but for one feature that captured my heart before I even stepped inside: the patio.

A white fence wrapped around the patio, with a wide gate that felt like an invitation to something special. It became my favorite part of the home, a small sanctuary where I could unwind and dream. Every morning, before heading off to work, I sat on the couch, closed my eyes, and pictured that gate swinging open, not just to the familiar sights of the townhouse complex, but to something far more enchanting. In my mind, beyond that gate lay a peaceful river, its waters glistening under the morning light, flowing endlessly toward the horizon. It was a quiet ritual, a moment of serenity before the day began, allowing me to escape, even if only in my imagination.

It wasn't long before I was sitting on my patio, sipping a glass of sweet tea, and planning my wedding. My mind wandered back to daddy's shop and Johnny Cash playing on the radio. I recalled asking to borrow Daddy's car and driving to the schoolyard where I would sing along to, "I Walk the Line".

I remembered that my first husband laughed out loud at the thought of dancing to my long since chosen song at our wedding. It took all the courage I had to barely whisper the words to my fiancé. Hey honey since I was a little girl I've always wanted the song for the first dance at my wedding to be "I Walk the Line". I held my breath wishing I had never opened my mouth I did not want another disappointment of someone laughing at one of my most precious and innocent childhood dreams. I knew at least he would take some time to think about it. As I braced myself for his answer, he looked up from his paper and without hesitation responded, "OK".

WEDDING DAT AT THE RIVER

On June 3rd, 2017. Jeff and I married on the banks of the Ohio River at the family vacation retreat where he spent summers with his parents and five brothers. Jim Dishman and Kelly played the music that enticed me onto the deck of Captain's Quarters the night we met. And now they played for our family and friends. And just as I imagined all those years ago, Jeff and I danced our first dance to the deep sultry voice of “my friend”, Johnny Cash singing, “I Walk the Line”.

Soon after we were married at the river house, it suffered one of the many floods it had seen. Jeff’s brother, who was living at the house at the time, was forced to leave until it could be cleaned up. He was at the home of a friend when he got up in the middle of the night. His friend heard him fall and found him at the bottom of the stairs. He had suffered a massive heart attack. Shortly after this, the river house was sold. I asked Jeff to keep it and move it into it, but he said he could not do another flood clean up. I spent a couple of nights there before it sold and cried the whole second day.

THE VIEW FROM OUR PATIO

I asked Jeff if he would consider a house on the river if I found one out of the flood plain. He said he would. I searched diligently. Houses on the river in our desired location and not in danger of flooding are a rare find. But I do not give up easily; rather, I do not give up. We made an offer on a house which was promptly rejected. The third offer, four months later, was accepted. We currently live in our own river house. It is home. It restores my soul daily. I thank God every day for letting us borrow it for a few years.

After we married, Jeff suddenly had several grandchildren, and he quickly learned the joys of being Paw. The day that Jeff and I were getting married, we were at the site about thirty minutes before the ceremony and Molli would not let go of him. She held his hand the entire time. At one point she looked up at Jeff and asked, "Will you take me swimming?" Jeff remarked, "Molli, I'm getting married in about twenty minutes!" Molli quickly responded, "I don't care a thing about this wedding, just take me swimming".

MY GRANDAUGHTER, LEXI

Lexi visited our home a month after our wedding. She rushed into the foyer and up the stairs to our living room, put her bags down, and gave me a big hug. As she started up the second set of stairs where Molli was waiting for her, she looked toward the recliner where Jeff was sitting and then back at me, her curiosity obvious. She could not see who was sitting there from where she was standing, so she made her way to the front of the chair. Seeing Jeff sitting there, she looked at me with increased curiosity and genuine surprise, and asked "Are you all still married?"

ALEX ALEX AND HIS DAD

We were having dinner one evening when I was visiting with Crystal and the kids. Just as we sat down at the dinner table, I asked the kids who wanted to say grace. Alex's dad walked by and rolled his eyes playfully. He did not subscribe to my beliefs. Looking up just in time to see his dad's reaction, Alex who was five years old at the time, in the maddest voice he could muster, yelled "Dad, there is a God! How do you think all of this got here?

MY GRANDDAUGHTER, AVA

One Christmas, all my kids and grandkids were at the house. It was about four o'clock and we had already had our Christmas dinner, so everyone was ready for a nap. Adam was trying to sleep, and Ava kept trying to wake him up. I told Ava to leave her daddy alone and let him sleep. She said that she needed to tell him something. I said, "Ava, can't you let daddy rest and tell him when he wakes up?" She turned to me with a look of concern not often seen in a child her age, "He needs to wake up or he won't sleep tonight". Trying to stifle a laugh, I asked "Ava, do you mind your daddy when you're at home?". She paused for a considerable amount of time before she responded, "Well I wove eem, all my haat.

MY GRANDCHILDREN, CONNOR AND ALIZABETH

When Connor was about four, he was giving Adam a lot of trouble. Adam sat him down and had a long talk with him, giving him a long list of changes he was expected to make including minding his sister when she was babysitting, writing on paper and not on the wall, refraining from saying bad words, cleaning up after himself, and flushing the toilet when he used it. After the conversation ended, Connor paused for a moment, looked at his dad with a serious expression, and said, “That’s too much.”

After Chris was shot and killed, my family met at Vickie’s home to ride together to the funeral home. When Crystal arrived with Layla and Molli, Molli ran straight over to me, crawled up on my lap, and gave me a big hug. Her arms still wrapped around my neck, she gave me a huge smile and announced, “Today’s the big day, Maw”

When Crystal was around eight years old, she was getting ready to go to bed. She was putting on her nightgown when she yelled at me in a voice that very seriously indicated that she wanted to show me something. I was curious and a little worried as she pulled up her nightgown and pulled up the edge of her panties. She had a huge boil right on her lower hip and upper leg she said, “Mama, tell me. “Do I have a hurby”.

Jeff also learned about the worry involved in being a grandparent. One evening we were watching TV when the phone rang. I hardly ever answered my phone unless I knew who it was, but for some reason, I just picked it up. It sounded strange, but the voice on the other line said, “Hey, Maw, it’s Layla.” As I was getting ready to reply, I heard her screaming. I also heard a lot of shuffling, and Layla yelling for me as she got further and further away from the phone. I dropped the phone and started screaming. I said somebody has Layla!!!!! The sound retreated away from the phone, a car door slammed, and tires screeched like someone was leaving, fast!

I was on the floor and couldn't get up. I was hysterical. I called Layla's phone over and over and got no answer. I finally called Crystal and asked her if she knew where Layla was. Crystal said, Layla was upstairs in the shower. I screamed at Crystal and told her to go up there and make sure she was in the shower. By now, the hysteria was beginning to spook Crystal, and she rushed upstairs and, sure enough, Layla was in the shower. She's in the shower! I am standing here talking to her. What in the world is wrong? I said I wanted to talk to her on the phone, and Crystal handed the phone to Layla. "I'm okay Maw." The three most beautiful words I ever heard. "What's wrong?" Layla continued. I dropped the phone and put my face in my hands and hit the floor again.

THE CLIMAX OF EVIL

"When an impure spirit comes out of a person, it goes through arid places seeking rest but does not find it. Then it says, 'I will return to the house I left." When it arrives, it finds the house unoccupied, swept clean, and put in order. Then it goes and takes with it seven more spirits more wicked than itself, and they go in and live there. And the final condition of that person is worse than the first."

Matthew 12:33-45 (NIV)

In early 1980s, a series of events that were set into motion by pure desperation, marked the beginning of the end. Mary was attending a church service when the congregation was invited to share prayer requests. After enduring years of escalating darkness surrounding Jerry's behavior, she made the decision to ask for prayer on his behalf. Though Jerry was not present, the group—comprised of devout and spiritually grounded Christians—joined together in a heartfelt and fervent prayer for his salvation and deliverance. There was no possible way he could have known that such a collective intercession had taken place. Unbelievably, in a few short weeks he started going to church and one day walked down the aisle and sought salvation. There was a great and immediate change in him. He stopped drinking and began attending church and Bible study regularly.

He seemed to be doing pretty well, and we were hopeful. It wasn't long, however, until he bought a King James Bible and refused to read or acknowledge the validity of the words in any other. He began to concentrate on the book of Revelation and the prophetic books in the Old Testament that elevated law over grace. He began to refer to himself as a prophet, specially chosen by God for a specific purpose that none of us could understand. But he was very judgmental and self-righteous and all but demanded that people recognize his special call and listen to him. Anyone who did not agree with his view of the Biblical call to service for God were doomed, as well as anyone who didn't profess that he was a super prophet with a special mission from God.

One evening, he set up a meeting with Wayne, my sister Mary's husband. Wayne was a Biblical scholar and had a college degree in philosophy and religion. He was a student of the Bible and a dynamic Christian apologist who would defend the teachings of Christ at any cost. When Jerry arrived, he was no longer the happy saved person that he seemed to be just a few weeks ago. He was very serious, and it was obvious that he had an agenda for this meeting. Mary told me that she felt that Jerry thought that because Wayne was a Biblical scholar, he would recognize Jerry's special calling, and he would have an ally in his mission.

Jerry solemnly started sharing with Wayne about his special calling and sharing details about why he was a prophet like no other. He was sharing his very skewed doctrinal beliefs when Wayne spoke. Wayne sat up on the edge of his chair, to have direct eye contact with Jerry. He asked, "Do you want to know my thoughts on this?" Not giving Jerry time to answer he stated unequivocally as he stared Jerry in the eyes. "You are deceived."

Jerry was furious! He made a few derogatory comments to Wayne and got up and left. He hated both Wayne and Mary from then on. This encounter with truth set him on a track to total loss of control and total dependence on evil to advance his self-proclaimed deity and to bring everyone he was around to their knees. At that time, it seemed that evil took complete control, and life was hell on earth to the ones who dared ~~to~~ not believe and especially to his family.

On a visit back home, when I went to check on Mama, I could tell immediately that something was terribly wrong. The moment I stepped into the kitchen, I saw it on her face—fear, pain, and an unbearable sadness. Her expression was strained, as if she were barely holding herself together, and the way she gripped the edge of the table made me uneasy. I started to ask her what was wrong, knowing I was likely to burst into tears if I opened my mouth. She just looked so lost, so hopeless. It even crossed my mind that she was dead sitting in her chair. It wasn't long before I understood.

A voice suddenly filled the air, a voice that sent a deep, chill down my spine. The hair raised on the back of my neck and my arms burned like I had been in the sun too long. This voice, distinctly different from any family member's voice, sounded unnatural, guttural, almost inhuman. Yet, impossibly, it was coming from Jerry. He was carrying on a conversation with himself in two entirely different voices. One voice was his own, familiar yet filled with fury, but the other—dark, diabolical, mocking—was something else entirely. The voices sometimes overlapped, speaking over each other, as if two beings were trapped inside Jerry's body, wrestling for control. The sinister voice would break into laughter at times, a slow, eerie chuckle that sent shivers down my spine. I listened in horror as the topic of their conversation became clear. They were discussing the details of killing Mama. Details I won't repeat.

My blood ran cold. The sheer agony on her face was unbearable to witness. I stood there, frozen, wishing more than anything that I could take away her pain and fear, but I was paralyzed. Suddenly, the doorknob turned. The voices stopped. A stillness filled the house that felt heavier than before. The door creaked open, and Jerry stepped out, his expression vacant. Now, he spoke only in his normal voice. But what happened next was even more disturbing. He slithered down to the floor like a snake, lying on his back, arching his shoulders, and throwing his head back unnaturally. His tongue flickered grotesquely, and his entire face contorted into something monstrous. His eyes rolled back into his head, and he writhed, twisting and jerking violently across the floor. The sight was horrifying, like he was possessed by something beyond human comprehension.

Occasionally, he would reach out and touch Mama, sending a visible shudder through her body. Her eyes were wide, her face drained of all color. Then, his voice changed again. He began speaking in tongues—wild, scattered, incoherent words spilling from his mouth like a fevered rant. But within the chaos, one phrase became clear. He was addressing Mama directly. He told her that he was Larry. He said he had come back to punish her for killing him. His words struck her like a dagger to the heart. She sat there, motionless, too devastated to react. Her breath was shallow, her hands trembling in her lap, but she did not cry. She just sat there, absorbing the horror, as if she had been expecting it all along.

I finally managed to convince her to leave the room, though she was, at first, hesitant, almost as if she feared what might happen if she abandoned him. But she followed me, and as quickly as this cruel torment had begun, it ended. The moment we stepped away, everything stopped. The writhing ceased, the voices silenced, and an eerie, suffocating quiet filled the air. It was as if none of it had ever happened. But I knew better. I knew that something dark had just unfolded before my eyes, something that would haunt me for the rest of my life.

Soon after this, I was spending the night at mama's and sleeping in my own bedroom. I was almost asleep when I heard a noise from the door. I looked up and Jerry was standing there in nothing but his underwear, his hands holding the trim over the door. He just stood there staring at me. Just to let him know how little he intimidated me. I just turned over in bed like I was going to sleep.

Linda shared an incident me with me that demonstrates the lengths Jerry would go to terrorize his family. We needed to go to the grocery store, but Mama wouldn't go. Normally, all three of us went together, but that day she stayed behind. Maybe she wasn't feeling well. I don't remember. When we got home, she was gone. We searched the whole house. Mama was always either at the kitchen table or on her couch. We called her name, but she was nowhere to be found. When we asked Jerry where Mama was, he just laughed.

We searched closets, under beds—everywhere. Finally, Jerry said with a smirk, "She is fine. She's dead out behind the garage." Daddy and I tore out the back door, screaming her name, running toward the garage but wanting to turn around and run in the opposite direction at the same time.

Before we got there, the next-door neighbor, Mama's only friend, opened her back door and called out, "She's over here." That was the only time I can remember Mama leaving home like that. She never told us what happened to make her leave, and I can only imagine what she must have suffered to feel an overwhelming need to escape. Soon after, Mama and Daddy took Jeff and me to stay with Vickie and her family for a while to get us out of the house. Jeff stayed longer than I did. I was in such bad shape that Vickie called Freelon for help. He took me to his home for a bit, but I eventually told him I just wanted to go home."

Linda shared ~~a~~another particularly chilling episode that turned out to be Jerry's last. For whatever reason, Jerry was worse than usual—like something possessed. He prowled back and forth, muttering, "It's all going to be over but the crying." "It's all going to be over but the crying." His eyes were piercing and filled with rage, his movements unnatural and unsettling. When he grabbed his car keys and stormed out, I felt the tiniest flicker of relief. I knew he was going for liquor, which meant things would turn even uglier, but at least we had time; time to breathe, time to prepare. But then, too soon, the growl of his engine cut through the silence.

He was back.

Mama and Daddy sat rigid, their faces filled with dread and resignation, the grim acceptance of what was coming. As he stomped up onto the porch, my mind went straight to the knives. I bolted to the kitchen, yanked them from their places, and shoved them deep into the trash, slipping the bag between the can and the liner. My hands shook as I hauled it out to the porch, praying he wouldn't notice. When he came through the door, the air turned thick with the stench of liquor. His eyes darted, hunting, feeding off the tension. Mama and Daddy didn't move, their silence an offering to whatever demon was driving him, delayed it.

His ominous energy had intensified. He began once again quoting the Book of Revelation, declaring that we would all bow to him. Daddy, trembling and helpless, was once again, begging him to stop. Jerry repeated his promise that the torment would end only after we submitted to him. Then, to my horror, our frail and terrified daddy, beaten down by years of fear, bowed before him.

He grew more ~~and more~~ frantic every minute, and he was calling himself, Larry, the Messiah, and even Jesus. He ranted about trying to save people, but people would not be saved. He kept hinting that something ~~really~~ bad was eminent. He finally revealed to Linda and me that that in order to fulfill his mission, he had to purchase a pint of whiskey to give him the courage to burn his former father in law's church, two relatively new church in Leitchfield, and large, and vibrant church in Custer. We had heard this type of threat so many times that we did not take him seriously. But after discussing it we decided to tell Freelon what Jerry had told us.

Freelon decided that he would go to the police in case just by some chance Jerry actually followed through. Freelon drove to the police station in Leitchfield and reported what we told him. The response was that the police could do nothing until Jerry broke the law. While Freelon was talking to the officer, the fire alarm went off. The fire department had to respond to a report that a church in Custer was burning.

Meanwhile, Mary got a call that the large Church in Custer had been burned, and it was a complete loss. Mary immediately called me to go get Mama and Daddy and Linda out of the house. She told me that Jerry had just burned a church, and she was afraid he would come to Mama and Daddy's and burn the house down with them in it.

Mama was not going to leave her house until I told her what Jerry had done and that he was on his way back to their house to set fire to it. When Mama heard this, she very quickly gathered a few things and came with me. As we all sat in my house, Linda told me that she, Mama, and Daddy had just gone to bed when I rushed in and told them to get up. She lay between them at the foot of the bed with a hand wrapped around their feet. She thought this might be the night that Jerry killed the three of them and she was sure that Mama and Daddy believed the same thing, but no one talked about it. Sadly, she had resigned herself to this fate.

Later that night, Jeff, our youngest brother, about fourteen at time, learned what had happened and came by my house. He and Linda clung to each other, both crying like babies. Linda told him between sobs "It is over. It is finally over." Imagine the sheer relief they felt after the years of torment and especially after the terror of the last several months as his behavior escalated.

Jerry burned one thriving church to the ground. He threw a Molotov cocktail into two more churches, but for some reason these went out without causing much damage. He drove to our old homeplace in Wax and burned two dilapidated shacks that we had played in our entire childhood. The old family house was already gone so he didn't have to burn it. He then drove to Veteran's Hospital in Louisville and turned himself in. Before he did, he parked his car under the awning of the entryway to the hospital and set it on fire which was arson directed towards a government building. He was arrested there and charged with first degree arson. After spending a short time in a mental hospital for evaluation, he served ten years in Luther Luckett Correctional Complex near LaGrange Kentucky.

While Jerry was away in prison, he somehow managed to write and send a letter to then-President Ronald Reagan. In this letter, he made an alarming threat, claiming that he was planning to assassinate the president, with the supposed help of my sister, Vickie, and my brother, Freelon.

It didn't take long for the letter to catch the attention of the authorities. Soon, the Secret Service arrived at my parents' house to investigate the situation. Mamma and Daddy, along with Freelon and Vickie, were questioned about their alleged involvement and any knowledge they might have had regarding his intentions. Of course, they were not involved at all, nor did they even know that Jerry had written such a letter.

I can only imagine the shock and fear that must have gripped my family when federal agents showed up at their doorstep, demanding answers to something so outrageous. Did they panic? Were they angry? Or did they simply shake their heads in exasperation, knowing all too well the troubled mind behind the accusation? Whatever their thoughts, I am confident that once again, they were thankful for the sense of safety they felt now, while still sorrowful for the future that Jerry would have to endure.

From what I've been able to piece together from my siblings—who have never been eager to discuss the incident—the conclusion was simple: "He's just crazy." It was an explanation both frustrating and familiar, a dismissal of his words as nothing more than the ramblings of an unstable mind. But whether the authorities truly believed that, or whether they continued to keep a quiet watch, remains unknown.

The lifting of a long-standing burden brought a sense of safety and relief to the family, offering the first chance in decades to sleep without fear. However, the trauma of more than forty years of constant fear left lasting effects on every member of the family. Even with the threat gone, its echoes remained. One night, years later, the scars of the past resurfaced when Linda woke abruptly to Jerry with his face right in hers screaming, "You better wake up! You better check on Mama and Daddy!" The traumatic memories of past fears were still deeply ingrained; showing that healing from such experiences is a long and ongoing process.

As I advance towards the end of my story, I know that there were ten other of my brothers and sisters who have their own story to tell. I want to give voice to their thoughts as well as my own. I asked my sisters, whom I spend a lot of time with for just a small part of their story. I asked them to share with you how the years of living in this intense fear, dread, and actual experience has affected their lives both then and now. Here is a ~~very~~ small part of each of their stories.

WORDS FROM THE SISTERS

Ann: As far back as I can remember in my childhood, I was always scared of everything. When I grew up, an engine revving was the cue to grab the little kids and run and hide. We spent hours hiding in the cornfield until we knew it was safe to go back to the house. Many nights I slept under the bed because I was so scared. Even now, sometimes I hear him whistling Greensleeves, which meant which was a bad omen. After everyone went to bed, he'd walk through the house whistling that over and over. It usually meant a bad episode was coming. It was creepy. Sometimes, he'd have a knife scraping the walls as he walked through the house whistling that song.

Janie: Jerry resented me because I stood up to him, and he hurt me multiple times. I knew that if I didn't leave home and get away from him, something bad would happen. So, at seventeen, I married a man who turned out to be a drunk and an abusive husband. After enduring that relationship for seven years, I finally broke free and swore that no man would ever lay a hand on me again. To this day, I have never fully trusted any man, despite being married four times. Now, at seventy-one, I don't dwell on the past. I am a strong, independent woman and I owe that to my past because while I bent, no one ever broke me.

Vickie: Growing up, the sound of revving engines terrified me. I always feared it meant Jerry was drunk. I developed a deep fear of enclosed spaces and still can't sleep in a bedroom with the door closed, a habit formed from all the times we hid in terrifying places to escape from him. In a way, those experiences made me stronger. I was determined that my own children would never know that kind of fear. But the past still lingers. I have lasting issues from the time Jerry hit me on the back with a platter when I was a teenager. The truth is, fear overshadowed my childhood. I spent most of it anxiously waiting for the next terrifying moment, never knowing when or what "it" would be. Even though I am stronger now, just writing this makes me tremble inside.

Mary: I remember the fear, apprehension, anxiety, and ceaseless worry that I would experience at various times when Jerry was in one of his volatile moods. When I was in about the third grade, I recall a sick, stomach squeezing, worry that I would carry around the entire day at school. I was worrying that there would be an "argument" going on when I got home from school. I would be truly sick all day in fearful expectation. I would go to Ann the very first thing when I got home and ask her, "Is there an argument going on?" I remember the tremendous relief that flooded me when she would say, "No." I would experience the same kind of worry and anticipation when I knew Jerry was in one of his "spells" and just wait for him to come into our room to hold a knife to my throat, shoot his gun through the ceiling, or another of the plethora of things he used to torture us and keep us soundly under his control.

There are many acts of evil that I remember Jerry doing to torment us but one stands out because of my reaction to it. I was very young, probably six or seven and we lived in Wax. Jerry was drunk and mad and just looking for a fight. Finally, something triggered him, and he went into one of his rages. He started yelling and screaming and throwing furniture etc. I cannot give the details because at the first sign that the rage was starting, I, a traumatized, terrorized six-year-old girl took off like a "bat out of hell". I ran out the back door in my bare feet like a long-distance runner and never slowed a single pace until I had run around the side of the house, past the apple tree, past the toilet, past the well, through a bunch of weeds and brambles and into a field of tall corn. I did not slow, nor did I look back until I was in the middle of that cornfield and far, far away from the danger zone. Every time I see or think about the scene in the movie "Forrest Gump", where the little girl is speed running through the corn field saying over and over, "Dear God, make me a bird so I can fly far, far, far away from here." [Zemmickis, R (Director) (1994) Forrest Gump (film) Paramount Pictures] I see an image of me running through that cornfield at the speed of light to try to escape the evil that was happening at home. After a while, I began to slowly make my way back home. When I got there everything was ok. Jerry was gone, and at least for now, there was blessed peace in the house.

The years of fear I experienced have had a lasting impact on me, shaping the way I navigate life today. I am fearful of the unknown. I feel extreme guilt if I hurt someone's feelings.

I lack confidence and am timid and unsure. I cannot stand to see others belittled or made fun of and if I have the opportunity, I will confront those responsible. I am especially kind and generous with my children and grandchildren, wanting to ensure they never experience the kind of pain I endured. Conflict unsettles me. I avoid arguments. I try to be good and uplifting to people. Because life is too short to dwell on painful memories, I choose not to think too much about my childhood. Instead, I focus on moving forward, doing good, and bringing kindness into the world.

Linda: I was terrified of Jerry, even after he was in prison. Even though he was locked up, I never doubted that he could walk through the door at any moment. I think that fear came from the countless times he was supposed to be locked in a mental hospital, yet he would show up at home within hours. Growing up in that violence conditioned me to accept things in my later years that I never should have allowed. I tolerated treatment from men that I shouldn't have because, in my mind, it wasn’t nearly as bad as my childhood. No one was ever very physically abusive to me, but I endured years of a different kind of abuse, mental and emotional.

I was his wife, and in his eyes, that made me his property. It took me years to understand that it was abuse. I know that many of my mental struggles stem from that torment. I spent most of my life afraid of everything. And I've carried guilt for thinking our parents were unfit for allowing us to live in constant fear. Jerry could hold a knife to our throats, and that was somehow acceptable, but Mary was beaten until her legs and back were raw just to make Mama stop hitting me. I lived in fear every single day of my life until I was about forty years old.

Tammy: As for me, a mismatched glass or cup or plate will send me into a rage. If I am in a room and someone closes the door, I will clear a table to get that door open. I will not position myself with my back to a door or an open area and will not set up a room where anyone can get between me and the exit. My bed must always be facing the door. I check out everyone in a room when I enter and notice any odd behavior instantly.

I sense when someone is upset with me before they know it and I don't have to see them. I can tell by a voice or footsteps. The older I get the more difficult it is for me to leave my house. If my husband asks me to go out to dinner, I silently cringe and if we have plans weeks ahead, I will be preoccupied with dread until it is over. When I am under stress, I feel only one thing can comfort me, and I am drawn to the furthest corner of a dark closet, wrapped in a cool quilt, hands covering my ears, praying.

I have great difficulty managing money. I have concluded recently that I am forever trying to fill the voids from childhood, to have my pantry filled with all the necessities; to have my cupboards, refrigerator, and aching belly full of food. I'm forever looking to satisfy that hunger and dull the pain of yearning for that pair of knee boots, the doll with the cloth body, the burgundy and tan sweater, the overalls all the other girls wore.

BREAKDOWN

During the last two or three years of my employment at Mariposa, I was slowly advancing towards dangerous territory. I was in a state where I was feeling totally responsible for all the hardships that I had endured and especially those suffered by my children. I was ~~in the process of~~ remodeling Adam's house, and I just couldn't do enough to make up for all the pain and hardship he had endured. My mind was a whirlwind that I could not control. And the whirlwind kept me from being able to think clearly and make reasonable decisions.

I was having difficulty remembering things and was falling behind in my paperwork. I began to have frequent and long-lasting panic attacks. Coming home from work one Wednesday, Jeff's dinner night with his friend, I knew I was going to be alone for some time. I was overcome by a feeling that is ~~very~~ difficult to describe. I can only explain the feeling as having a great need to be around people who liked me. That was the recurring thought.

I went to Captain's Quarters where I could listen to some live music and hopefully see some familiar faces, thinking it might settle my nerves. Listening to the band, my emotions were erratic and unsettling. My mood shifted from sad to angry to feeling guilty for the anger. I realized that I had made an unwise decision by stopping there. I gathered my things to leave, but when I tried to stand, my body refused to move. I was in the grip of a full-blown panic attack—frozen, unable to follow through on the simple command to get up. For twenty long minutes, I sat there, hoping one of the servers would notice and come to my aid. Finally, a bartender made eye contact with me. From across the room, she asked if I was okay. All I could do was barely shake my head. She rushed over and put her hand on my back and asked what was wrong. I could barely get out a quite squeaky "panic attack".

She began rubbing my back, urging me to take deep breaths and count with her. Slowly, I felt the panic subside, whatever was immobilizing my body was loosening its grip, and I was able to move. Once I could move again, she told me to stay put. She was calling my husband to get me. But as soon as she stepped outside, I found myself getting up and walking to my car. I was not planning to drive off. I just needed fresh air and a moment of quiet. Sitting there, I replayed the scene in my mind, embarrassed by the commotion I had caused and struggling to regain my composure.

Minutes later, my husband pulled up. He gently helped me out of my car and into his and we headed toward home. Once we arrived, he tucked me into bed, his steady presence offering some sense of safety. The next morning, I had a telehealth appointment with my psychiatrist. When I woke up, I realized I only had a few minutes to get downstairs, log onto my computer, and prepare for the session. That realization alone sent me spiraling into another panic attack.

The moment my doctor's face appeared on the screen, I burst into tears, choking out the story of what had happened the night before. We talked about scheduling therapy to address the root of these recent escalations of panic. When the session ended, I called my sister, Mary. Hearing her voice grounded me, and I asked if she could come stay with me for a few days. She arrived that evening, and on the second day, I worked up the courage to ask her for something more.

"Can you help me find a place to go? Somewhere where I can receive intensive inpatient therapy, somewhere I can really get help". Mary did not hesitate. She started researching options at once. I messaged Jim to ask if taking time off work would jeopardize my job. His reply was swift and certain: Absolutely not! That night, I packed my bags, unsure of what lay ahead but determined to find a way out of the darkness. By midnight, I was on my way to a mental rehabilitation center, clinging to the hope that this was the beginning of something better.

Intake was overwhelming and disorienting. All my regular medications were confiscated and locked away because I had packed them in unmarked containers. I did not argue. I trusted their process. They assured me my prescriptions would be reordered the next morning, so I could stay on schedule. That reassurance carried me through the first day. But by the fourth day, I still had not received them. I was taking some medications that have strong withdrawal symptoms, and I was feeling them. I felt I was on the precipice of a complete collapse.

By day five, I reached my breaking point. I begged to call home, just to hear a familiar voice. But the answer was always no. You need your therapist present for phone calls, they told me. I felt cut off from the outside world, isolated with no relief in sight. Desperation clawed at me.

Without my medication, my body rebelled. My skin prickled and crawled as if something was living beneath it. Nightmares crept into my sleep. A pounding headache was constant. My anxiety skyrocketed, leaving me unable to focus or breathe normally. I was unable to stop crying. I felt like a prisoner in my own mind, unable to quiet the tics that had begun to surface. Each day, I would ask, when will my meds be here? And each day, I would get the same apology. They will probably be here tomorrow.

I went to one of the technicians and asked her to arrange a meeting with a case manager so that I could call home. Soon after, I was invited into the office of the on- call case manager. She handed me my phone. I began to dial Mary's number. The case manager quickly stood and was coming around her desk, "I can't let you make a phone call. You must do that with a therapist, just put your name on the board outside their offices." "I did that four days ago." I responded. By this time, I was done with the rules. "And you can't stop me from making a phone call." I replied. "But I won't yet. I thought that was why we were here." She told me I was there to place an Amazon order and that she would contact the on-call therapist and ask her to see me. I agreed to place the order and waited for the therapist before I made a phone call. As she entered God knows what on her keyboard, I placed my order, or so she thought. I quickly sent Mary a text message “Please come get me”. She asked for the address, and I responded, “No time. Call Jeff and ask him to call and demand to speak to me”.

When my therapist finally called me into her office, I told her everything. The withdrawals. The excuses. The isolation. I explained how I had reached my limit and could not endure another minute. I need somewhere to recover from this recovery, I said, my voice cracking. This place has done more damage to me in five days than I have experienced since my sister died. It was not the kind of healing I had come looking for.

I was at the therapist’s office no more than five minutes when someone pounded on the door. The therapist opened the door to the Nurse Practitioner who asked her to come outside and started to close the door. “If you are going to talk about me, do not shut the door to keep me from hearing you, that creates distrust, and I would think you would know that”. He ignored me and shut the door. Linda returned promptly, laughing. “They want to know if you have a phone on you. The nurse practitioner stood, waiting for an answer. I stood, spread out my arms, and responded, “Why don’t you come find out for yourself?” I then added “Are you by any chance wondering why my husband called? I texted him when you thought I was placing an Amazon order.”

When I returned home, I resumed my medication and felt slightly better, but within days, weakness overwhelmed me. I had eaten almost nothing in the previous ten days and could only drink milk, which at least put some nutrition in me. I could not get off the couch, and after two more days, I told my husband I needed to go to the ER. When I arrived at the ER, I was rushed back to a room. They ran bloodwork, EKG, chest X-ray and gave me heated blankets, though I was still freezing under five layers. An IV helped, but my blood pressure and temperature were dangerously low.

My husband asked about seeing a psychiatrist, and within forty-five minutes, she arrived. Her assessment led to intensive outpatient therapy, five days a week. I started three days later. For six weeks, I found healing, wonderful therapists, and unexpected friendships. Now, four of us who met at those therapy sessions meet monthly for brunch. We are four women who would never have crossed paths otherwise but now share a bond we will always cherish.

REST IN PEACE

Mama died April 8, 1992, in her home. Mama had been a smoker her whole life. I went to visit her one weekend and she told me she had quit smoking. I knew something was wrong when she told me this. I spoke with some of my sisters, and they too were concerned. They spoke to Mama about going to the doctor and she agreed. She was diagnosed with stage four lung cancer that had metastasized to her bones. She refused treatment and took the news that she only had a few weeks left with grace and courage. My sisters and I began clearing our calendars in order to spend every second we could with her. Mama lived for seven weeks after her diagnosis. Her daughters spent most of that time sitting around her bed during the day and taking shifts to care for her at night. My sisters were kind enough to leave me out of the rotation. A reflection of my love language, I took and the task of assuring everyone was well fed. My skills lie in caring for the caregiver. The tender and meticulous treatment of the dying is beyond my capacity.

When mama was dying, she didn't protest or complain. She didn't express any fear about dying until one evening when all ~~of~~ her girls were sitting with her. Out of the blue she started crying. It broke our hearts to see Mama so small and frail lying in her bed, overcome by such sadness. Mary gently asked her, "What's wrong Mama?", moving to the bed to hold her hand. Mama responded in a child-like voice, which was heartbreaking to all of us, "I don't want to die." She paused for a few seconds and said, "He's going to hurt my girls." Nobody asked her who she was talking about because we knew. We did not want her to be afraid and we did not want to add to her sadness. The next morning, she called us all into her room. "I want to tell you girls something. What I said yesterday about not wanting to die, don't you pay attention to that." She continued, "I didn't mean it. It was just the drugs I'm taking. And I don't want you girls to think I'm afraid."

The sisters continued to take shifts staying in the room with mama. One night, Ann was sitting with her, the rest of us sleeping wherever we could find a spot. Ann was so tired that she nodded off for a few minutes. When she awoke, Mama had passed away. Ann woke Mary and said, "I think she is gone." Mary confirmed mama's death and woke us and reported "Mama has died."

That night after she had been taken from the house, all us girls were in one room trying to fall asleep when I started laughing uncontrollably. I kept trying to get the words out to no avail. Finally, I blurted out, still laughing hysterically, "Mary, are you sure she was dead?" Janie responded, "Oh Lord Tammy, go to sleep." Mary peeped up very quietly, "Well, I think she was." That did it, I was laughing again until my whole body hurt and then slowly my laughter turned into sobs. As I said, it's something I don't do well. Mama loved well and was well loved during her last days!

After Mama died, I had a most disturbing dream about her. My sisters had called the funeral home to come and take mama away. Later we were cleaning up her room when it occurred to me that we forgot to speak to the coroner, leaving us afraid that she was not dead, and that she was in the funeral home alone wondering why she was there. I decided to walk up to the funeral home to check on her. There was no one there because it was the middle of the night, but I of course had a key to the front door. I searched the building, room after room, until I found a room with a dim light on. I could barely see a small body lying on an embalming table.

The body was covered in a white sheet, but I knew it was mama because one arm was hanging off the table. I recognized her long slender fingers that I had watched, so many times, guide the fabric that would be one of my garments through the foot of her sewing machine. The hand that had so gently rested on my forehead to check for a temperature and then lingered to comfort a sick child, the long fingernails she inspected mindlessly to avoid looking into the eyes of her oldest son.

I walked over to the table and pulled the sheet back and there was my sweet mama, eyes wide open and staring back at me. I was unfazed by her looking at me but relieved that I could go back and tell my sisters to rest assured that we had not left Mama alive, awake, and alone in a dark room.

I carefully covered her back up taking care to put her arm back under the sheet because Mama was always cold. I turned around to leave the room rehearsing what I was going to tell my sisters. As I reached to open the door, I heard a terrible thud coming from the direction of the table where Mama lay. I looked back and saw Mama lying on the floor face down. I went back to her and turned her over and tried to lift her back onto the table and cover her up because I didn't want her to be cold. After several attempts to lift her. I realized I was going to have to leave her on the floor, so I took the sheet off the embalming table and covered her up. She continued to stare right at me.

I stood and again started toward the door, but I didn't leave. I knelt back down beside her and just stared at her open eyes for a while. I stroked her forehead a few times. I gripped her bottom jaw with my left hand and her top jaw with my right began to pull until her bones started cracking. Occasionally, I would feel a sharp bone piercing my hand, but I kept going until her jaw was lying on her on her chest. I stood up, wiped my hands on my pants and looked down at Mama and said, "Next time do better."

I had always had nightmares and very violent ones, but I had never had a dream where I was the one committing the violence. I never had any animosity toward my mother. Or maybe I, like many others, wondered why she and Daddy allowed their children to suffer such abuse for so long.

Chris died ~~on~~ December 9, 2015—the day of his wife, Connie's birthday and just one day before my own. I was at work when my phone rang. It was my daughter. Her voice was cautious and gentle, as if she were carefully choosing each word. She hesitated for a moment before telling me she had some bad news. My grandchildren were the first thing that popped into my mind. "Please tell me the kids are okay". "It's not the kids Mama. I just saw on social media that Uncle Chris was shot by a police officer. I asked, "Well, is he okay". Her response, barely audible was "No Mama". I wanted to scream but I had a patient in front of me. I motioned to a coworker to keep her eyes on him, and I ran out of the room.

My mind wandered to sweet Chris, playing the guitar, asking me to sing, "I Shall Not Be Moved", and telling me I had the voice of an angel. I remembered him messaging us all when it snowed, "Do not forget to feed the birds". I could see him standing there, his salt and pepper beard hiding a never-ending smile, always looking as if he were deep in thought. I could feel a scream crawling up my throat again, but I knew I had to maintain control until I got out of the building. What was the possible reason for this tragedy? Why would anyone want to harm dear, sweet Chris? And a police officer, of all people! Chris never broke a law in his life.

Chris, who was known far and wide for his kindness, honesty, and gentle spirit. What in the world? He was shot in his own front yard, killed by a police officer in what was ultimately judged to be suicide by cop. The trauma of his divorce, the strife within his family, walking away from his beloved home, the weight of life had all become too much for him to bear. Despite being so loved by his family, such a treasure to his sisters and brothers, Chris could no longer bear what life had dealt him. He chose death, leaving us all with nothing but memories.

The officer who shot my brother was a friend of one of our siblings. He later spoke with Linda, expressing the deep regret he felt for what he had to do. He recounted the day's events, and this is how my dear sweet brother died. The police were called to a domestic violence claim at my brother's address. Chris was locked out of the house and carrying a firearm. He approached the police officer, raised the gun and pointed it directly at the officer's face. The officer repeatedly ordered him to drop his weapon. Chris continued to approach him, gun raised. He was shot in the chest and according to the officer, he did not suffer. My brother was shot by a policeman, but the officer was not responsible for his death. He was merely the weapon. Chris's death was orchestrated long before.

Connie and the stepson were allowed to live in the house that Chris put his heart and soul into. Chris's biological children, who loved their dad dearly and were loved by him, had no claim to their dad's property.

ANN AND JERRY

A few months after Chris's death, Social Services was called to the home where Connie still lived with their adopted son. A neighbor had seen some things that concerned her. What they found was unimaginable.

Connie was crouched under the kitchen table, covered in feces, and begging for food. As the police officers walked her out, she begged them for food and added, please not "baloney". To imagine Chris seeing his wife of forty-four years being led out of the house they shared together in such a condition is unbearable. Chris treated stray dogs better than his wife was treated after he was no longer there to protect her.

JANIE, JERRY, AND LINDA

When Chris was killed. Linda called Jerry in Florida to let him know. She told him we were having a memorial at Mary's house. I am sure it had to take every ounce of courage he could muster to ask if she thought any of the family would mind if he came to the memorial. She assured him no one would mind; that the family would be glad to see him. She had no idea, of course, how the family would receive Jerry, but Linda was always the kind one and at worst, anyone who didn't want to see him could stay away. I had not spoken to him in almost thirty years and for many of those years I saw him every day. Our younger brothers did not attend the memorial. I believe it was just too difficult for them. All the sisters were there and a lot of our children. And Jerry.

JERRY AND LINDA AT HIS HOME IN FLORIDA

We gathered for a meal and sat at the kitchen table, surrounded by boxes of old photos. We talked, laughed, and cried. The home was filled with nostalgia and weeping . The air was thick, but not with fear, not with anger, not with evil, but with forgiveness. Jerry was different this time. Whatever he had carried back from Vietnam, that haunted and ~~had~~ ravaged my family for fifty years, was not with him now. He was humbled. Though he never said it aloud, he was sorry. In that room, surrounded by people who had suffered under his reign of terror, he was forgiven. There was no evil left, no anger or resentment. Only peace, grace, and the quiet understanding hearts that had healed from their shared pain.

JERRY AT HOME IN FLORIDA

In 2021, Romey passed away, leaving behind a mobile home setting on a modest piece of land that his father had willed to him many years before. After his passing, his siblings agreed to sell the property to me for a very reasonable price. I, in turn, sold it to Adam on a monthly payment plan. When his dad and I divorced in 1987, the court had awarded me a $75,000 judgment against Romey, a sum I never saw. Decades later, in 2021, it became symbolic as I purchased this home for Adam valued at $70,000, though I was able to buy it for much less. The home needed extensive repairs, so my sisters and I spent weekends working on it.

ADAM

Adam saw the property as more than just a place to live; it was a chance to rebuild, to lay down roots. Soon after Adam moved in, my sisters and I spent our weekends at the home with the intention of working on some repairs to ensure the place was safe and warm for Adam and his three children. Before the job was completed, we had basically gutted the whole house and replaced floors and cabinets, appliances and furniture. We built porches and added a room. Adam had a home for the first time in his adult life.

One day in late summer, I happened to be working alone. I was crouched on the floor, hammering loose boards back into place. I was deep in thought, my mind on the work before me, when I felt it—a presence at my left shoulder. It wasn't alarming or cold; rather, it was gentle and unmistakably familiar. It wasn't just a feeling; it was an energy, a quiet yet undeniable presence. I froze, my heart skipping a beat. Without a doubt, I knew it was Romey. For a moment, I sat there, unsure of what to do. My chest tightened, not out of fear but from an overwhelming wave of emotion. The presence lingered, steady and watchful, as though Romey had been waiting for this moment to communicate with me. I set the hammer down softly, wiping my hands on my jeans, and turned to my left.

The room was still, and quiet, the last of the evening light warming my face. I was alone, yet not alone. I swallowed hard and spoke softly, almost instinctively. "Romey," I said, trying to find the right words. "You don't have to worry anymore. Everything is forgiven." The presence lifted, dissipating like a gentle breeze, leaving behind a profound sense of peace. The silence that followed was not empty. It was full, rich with the feeling of release and resolution. I sat there for a while, staring at the space where I'd felt him, my heart both heavy and light at the same time.

Jerry passed away in March 2024; Jerry had moved back to Kentucky to stay with his daughter. The doctors told him If he wished to die at home, he best head towards home. Jerry died with three of his four children and three of his sisters at his side. They lovingly cared for him during his last days. I went to the house one day to prepare a meal for all of them but was not able to sit in the room with him or tell him goodbye. Too many emotions ran through my head. None of them hate. I just could not do it. I had so many questions about what must be going through his mind.

My brother was sick. He was diagnosed after he left home with paranoid schizophrenia. I will wonder as long as my mind can think, if that disease was the root cause of all the years of turmoil. I hope it was. I prefer to believe that Jerry was sick and am reviled at the possibility that he was just evil! I choose to believe that he had good in him the whole time, just fighting to get out. I choose to believe that in the end he made a conscious choice to pursue good over evil. I choose to believe that Jerry is resting peacefully now.

EPILOGUE

I don't claim to be an expert on mental illness—but I *am* an expert on mine. I've battled it in one form or another since grade school. While other children were learning to sound out words in picture books, I was learning to decipher the language of tightening fists, dilated pupils, flared nostrils, and darting glances. My brain learned early to stay alert, to pay attention in ways most people never have to.

Doubting my worth, I married the first man who showed interest, thinking that was what I was supposed to do. I survived through four years of betrayal and brutality, clinging to what I'd thought it meant to be a good wife: that a woman's job was to endure, to meet others' needs, and to stay quiet. When I was sexually assaulted—more than once—I didn't even feel anger. It hardly registered. It was just another thing to carry. Another silent weight added to all the others.

Sometimes I feel unstoppable, driven by the need to fix, to clean, to repair—anything to avoid surrendering to sleep. Time wasted must be made up. Other times, I'm nearly helpless, paralyzed by the simplest tasks: taking medication, mailing a letter, returning a call, sorting socks, making a bed. The night, with its stillness and its freedom from judgment, is my sanctuary.

My past clings to me like smoke—dark, thick and threatening to steal my breath. Witnessing cruelty toward the vulnerable, leaves me fearless in their defense. My past has shaped my present and my future. Poverty was more than a condition, it was a smothering existence, and while I know my family isn't the only one that lived with its suffocating weight, it left a lasting imprint. No matter how far I climb, its grip tries to pull me back. Some families share stories like mine. But not many can say they grew up in a home occupied by evil.

We did.

Evil was real to us, as real as Mama's love and Daddy's labor and the bruises left on my sisters. We didn't just believe in it, we *knew* it. If you don't believe in evil, then you never felt it standing silently at the foot of your bed, thickening the air until you couldn't breathe. You didn't see it twist a body into inhuman shapes, hear two voices speak from the same throat, or witness it describe to your Mama what fire does to a child's skin. You didn't wake to a knife blade dragging across the floor or feel it's cold edge stinging as it pressed against the skin of your neck. You didn't see children deprived of food, flung across a room, held over burners, or under cold water. You had the luxury of not believing.

We didn't.

Most of what I've shared in this book has been hard to write. These are stories we never wanted to tell. But I brought them out of the dark, into the light—not for sympathy, not for shame—but for freedom. Healing has come through telling the truth, through speaking aloud what once stayed locked inside. I know this book has the potential to either draw criticism or compassion. My hope is that it brings someone else comfort—enough to know they're not alone, and that they're not without hope.

Today, I cherish these things: the quiet luxury of matching furniture, the crispness of clean sheets, the soft glow of sunlight pouring through my windows. I feel peace when I open a cabinet and find clear matching glasses in a neat row. I'm grateful for fresh running water—for drinking and bathing, for the simple miracle of turning a faucet and being blessed with water. My pantry holds food. My bed is warm. I am beyond fortunate.

Sometimes I picture that little girl who stands in front of our tiny house in Wax, Kentucky. She smiles softly as she sits on the edge of my bed and watches in quiet wonder as I style my hair and apply my makeup. She patiently waits for me to open the closet door. Jumping down from the bed, she runs toward me, and gently squeezing my hand, she stares in amazement at the bright colors, neatly pressed, and arranged on matching hangers. I wish I could go back —to tell her she made it. But going back is not the answer. So, as she slowly— step by step, makes her way toward me, I wait for her, wrapped in the comfort of knowing that I am home. I am safe. And I am not afraid.

The End

Made in the USA
Columbia, SC
01 July 2025

fa559d07-e1b8-4e5c-b41a-75f864a85c7eR01